MW01680172

The Snappin Sistas

Present

SECRET SPOTS FOR PHOTO OPS

In Missouri and Illinois

A zaney non-tourist travel guide to unusual places that are within 150 miles of Downtown St. Louis

The Mis-Adventures of Judy, Nancy and Angie
Written by Judy Coday

Copyright © 2013 by Judy Coday, Nancy Lister and Angie Gellner

ISBN: 978-1-891442-95-7

Price (retail): $24.95

To order additional copies of this book go to www.snappinsistas.com

All rights reserved. No part of this book may be reproduced in any form or by any electronic or mechanical means, including information storage or retrieval systems, without permission in writing from the publisher, except by a reviewer, who may quote brief passages in review.

Edited by: Penny Taylor
Designed by: Angie Gellner

Bluebird Publishing Co.
St. Louis, MO 63144
www.bluebirdbookpub.com

We dedicate this book to our wild and crazy guys,
Bill, Tom and Dave.
Thanks for your support, love and money!

ACKNOWLEDGMENTS

We want to also thank the following people who have helped us along the way.

Laura Edwards Ray, a new BFF and author, who willingly shared her information and trade secrets of the book writing/publishing world.

Bill Coday, my husband and lifetime friend, who listened to my endless nattering about the book, and voluntarily fed the horses, cats and dog while I was off exploring with my sistas.

Michelle Blumenthal, another BFF and friend for life, who requested to be the first person to buy a book.

Kymberlieblu Birkenkamp, my Shutter Club buddy, who patiently gave us more than helpful marketing advice.

Penny Taylor, our editor, who diligently plowed through this book and corrected all of the mistakes.

TABLE OF CONTENTS

Chapter 1 Introduction..1

Chapter 2 Getting Started 7
Lens Envy 9
No Unsafe Places 10
Pit Stops...12
What About Shooting People on the Street (Camera) 15

Missouri Destinations

Chapter 3 Reed Spring Mill 31

Chapter 4 Callaway Fork Road 34

Chapter 5 Missouri Mines State Historic Site 38

Chapter 6 Black Madonna Shrine..................................43

Chapter 7 Riverside Wildlife Ranch 45

Chapter 8 DeSoto 49

Chapter 9 Valles Mines 56

Chapter 10 Daniel Boone Home 61

Chapter 11 Femme Osage 64

Chapter 12 Defiance...68

Chapter 13 Caledonia...73

Chapter 14 Potosi 77

Chapter 15 Downtown St. Louis 80

Chapter 16 Crown Ridge Tiger Sanctuary 86

Chapter 17 Clarksville 89

Illinois Destinations

Chapter 18 River Overlook 95

Chapter 19 Riverlands Migratory Bird Sanctuary....................97

Chapter 20 Grafton....................100

Chapter 21 Elsah....................103

Chapter 22 Principia College....................106

Chapter 23 Alto Pass 108

Chapter 24 Maeystown....................113

Chapter 25 Prairie du Rocher and Chester....................115

Chapter 26 Arthur....................120

Chapter 27 How to Be A Moron With or Without a Camera....................127

Chapter 28 What To Do With All Those Photographs ...133

Chapter 29 Tips for the Aspiring Photographer....................145
Exposure Tips 148
Books, Software, Magazines, Websites, Classes, Clubs....................149

Chapter 30 Tips and Favorite Places to Shoot From the St. Louis Pros 152

Chapter 31 Where to Go When the Weather Won't Cooperate....................160

Topic Index Ideas and Additional Places to Shoot 168

Parks County and State Great Photo Ops 176

HOW TO CONTACT US....................179

ONE

INTRODUCTION

If you are a dreadfully serious person like my husband, Bill, put this book down. It's not for you.

We – the Snappin Sistas – are three rather wacky, fun-loving friends who love getting together (practically every weekend with cameras in tow) and we want to share the charm and maybe-never-heard-of destinations of the areas we have visited in Missouri and Illinois (all within 150 miles of downtown St. Louis).

You don't have to be a photographer to enjoy this book. If you just love getting out for an hour or all day, this book will help you discover those secret, out-of-the-way places around our area.

I want to introduce us so you will understand where the content and sometimes off-the-wall, light-hearted comments about exploring and photography originated.

SHAMELESS SELF PROMOTION

We are camera and road trip addicts, not even trying to recover. It's a high, a hobby, a love and sometimes we even make money. But money wasn't our goal when we started hanging out together. We just wanted to get out, explore and better our photography skills. You know the statement "the more you shoot, the better you become" saying? We even dream about our next shoot or lie awake at night planning how we might frame something or someone and shoot it. Sick, huh? We know there are plenty of you out there doing the same thing, as evidenced by the meet-up groups, camera clubs and people we meet out on the road. We live to hear someone say, "Wow, that's awesome. Where did you take it?" By now, you are saying, "Wow, they really are demented." Nevertheless, we know we are not alone.

Meet The Snappin Sistas

"Bad Nancy"

She is really Nancy Lister and here's how "Bad Nancy" earned her nickname.

We met about eight years ago in a photo class given by an older gentleman named Art, a kind and generous man, and a great photographer. Nancy was not named "Bad Nancy" back then.

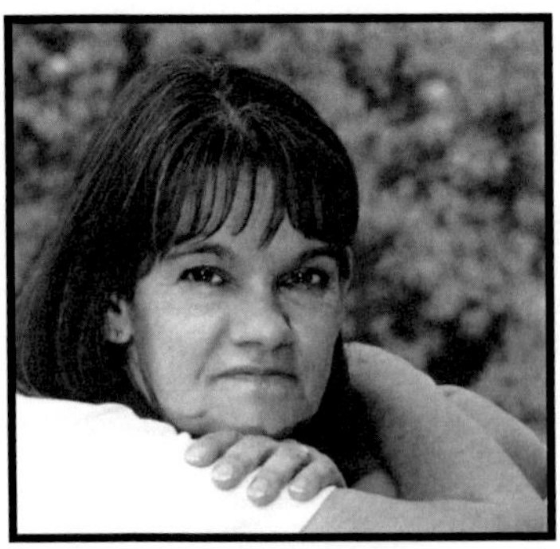

During one of these classes, Art asked me to bring my tripod up to the front of the class so he could show us how to level our tripod legs. I was struggling to get the tripod legs open and Art, in all innocence, instructed me to "quit spreading my legs first, but to keep them together." I tried to smother a giggle, but I heard snickering coming from the second row. I looked up and spotted a woman, shoulders shaking and trying hard to suppress giggles. Never being able to resist an audience or an opening, I muttered "Maybe I would have been more popular in high school if I had **NOT** followed that advice." A few other class members burst out laughing and Art, always the gentleman, reddened, and changed the subject. Too late. I knew I would like that woman and we would become fast friends. We did. She has many other incidents I won't mention here that motivated me to call her "Bad Nancy" so I could differentiate between her and another mutual friend named Good Nancy.

Bad Nancy is a firecracker with an endless capacity for seeing the humorous side of life and for putting up with my endless questions about Photoshop. I would have given up years ago if I didn't have her tutoring me every step of the way. She is always willing to help anyone – friend, family or stranger.

"Fearless Angie"

Angie Gellner we nicknamed "Fearless Angie." Here's how she earned that nickname.

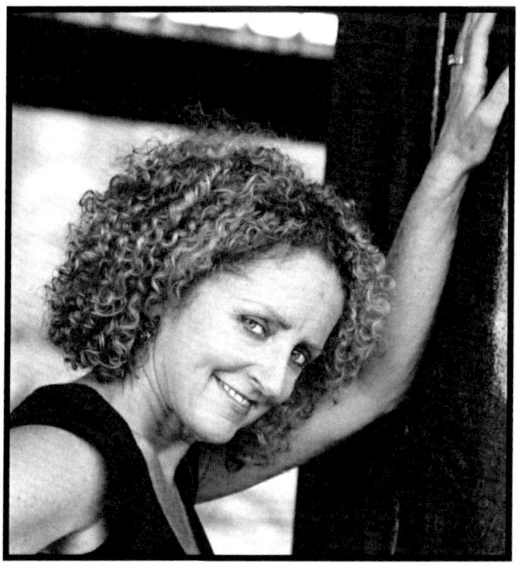

Angie shares my love of horses (Nancy prefers a car) and since I have two horses and she expressed an interest in riding, I put her on my big Belgian Paint, Joejoe. Being the "Riding Instructor of the Year," I told her to hang on since Keely (my Arabian horse and general bad boy) was anxiously waiting to charge off. Joejoe, following close on Keely's heels, did his usual bucking and farting (not big bucks but farts are another thing) and I could hear Angie behind me laughing hysterically at his antics and she not only hung on, she STAYED ON, like in-the-saddle-on. I knew she would because she has what we horse people call a "good, natural seat." Aren't you impressed? I was.

I think Angie grew up as the kid other kids, who didn't want to get in trouble but wanted the thrill of saying they were in on the escapade, would say, "Let's get Angie to do it." As far as we know, she didn't resort to criminal activity but she does exhibit the "no fear" attitude. This woman owns her own chain saw and table saw, for heavens sake, and thinks nothing of taking down big trees behind her house.

She gives Nancy and I courage to break out of the mold and go where no man has gone before! We do, however, let her go first and check out deserted buildings before the two of us venture in. We hate to look like sissies, but she's so darn cute we know she could talk her way out of anything. With her head of curly hair and an addiction to adventure, we love her, when not muttering under our jealous, collective breaths, "That bitch. Doesn't she ever put on weight?" while she wolfs down a man-sized sandwich AND dessert.

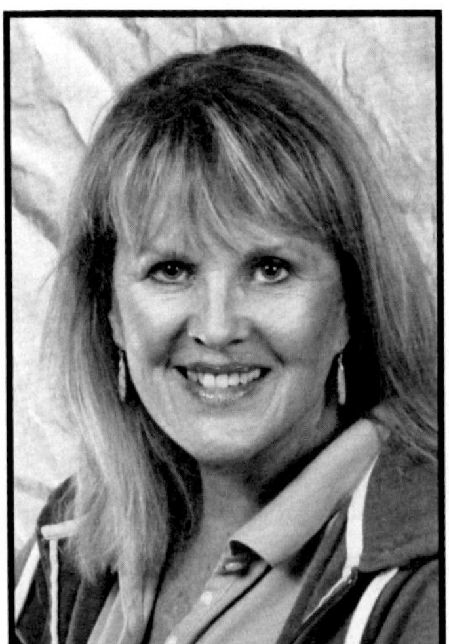

"Cowgirl Judy"

Me? I'm Judy Coday and I don't know what the other two call me behind my back (probably Gestapo Bitch). I'm a recovering co-dependent and co-dependents like to CONTROL. I am the planner, organizer and follower, all in one. Oh, and I will mention it before anyone else does – I am the oldest, but young in spirit. I hate mirrors – they lie. I know I am still 36. Why don't I look like it? Since I grew up with a cowboy for a father and still ride my horses, I received the nickname of Cowgirl Judy.

Like the other two, I have a wicked sense of humor and am totally addicted to photography.

We all have husbands who play golf and grown children, so we have the luxury of free time on the weekends. Our men are perfectly happy if we head out on a road trip, as long as their laundry is done before we leave. Just Kidding. I'm sure the other two husbands figured out long ago, like mine did, to buy lots of extra pairs of underwear so they can get through three or more weeks. They are really good sports about our addiction. Personally, we think they are relieved they don't have to go with us on photoshoots. On the rare occasions when they have accompanied us, we have heard, one too many times, "How many pictures are going to take of that dead tree?"

Only true camera nuts can understand each other's addiction.

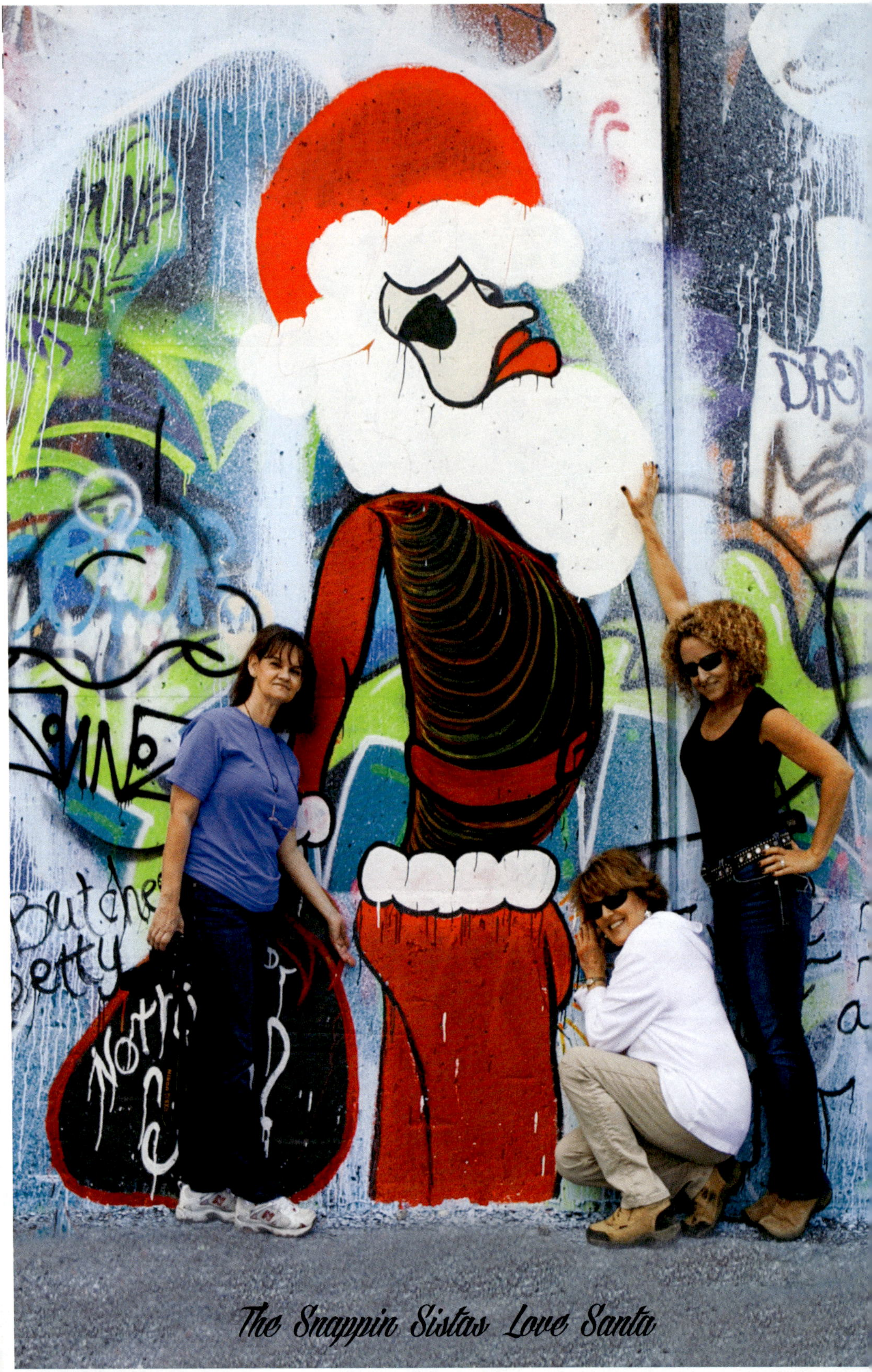

The Snappin Sistas Love Santa

TWO

GETTING STARTED

We've done all the work for you. In our quest for adventure, we've purchased lots of guidebooks but most do not contain those out-of-the-way, unusual spots that those of us with cameras love to show off pictures of and hear our friends say, "Where did you take that?" You can now smugly say, "I discovered this place."

This book is different. Of all the guidebooks we've looked at, most contain either too much overwhelming information or lots of restaurants and shopping areas. We are certainly not against eating and shopping. Just take a look at our waistlines – okay – two of us have that problem and the other runs three to five miles a day. We hate her and talk about her behind her back.

This is a handy guide because we are sharing some of our favorite, weird, and scenic spots along with the following:

- Approximate mileage from St. Louis City
- Easy directions, fun descriptions, and photographs
- Food availability
- Handicap accessibility

If adventure and seeing out-of-the-way-places-never-mentioned-in-most-travel-books is your calling, come with us as we explore Missouri and Illinois.

LENS ENVY

While it's true that not all people are friendly, we will tell you that we have found fellow photographers to be the friendliest of the friendly and more than willing to help you. So, if you see someone dragging around a camera, along with a lot of equipment, don't be afraid to approach them if you need help, or even if you just want to ask them about their equipment. Why do you think we carry all that stuff around?

Truly, it doesn't matter what kind of camera equipment you have. We have seen amazing shots come out of cell phones and if that's all you have, so what. Shoot away. It's your interest and intent that count.

And, don't be fooled by people with big lenses on their cameras. They are just like the rest of us. We do admit to lens envy from time to time, losing our cool demeanor when we see a guy, particularly at the zoo, with a humongous lens on his camera body. We've said many times while drooling with envy, "WOW. What kind of a lens is that? It's HUGE."

Sorry, we just can't help ourselves and read into that what you will.

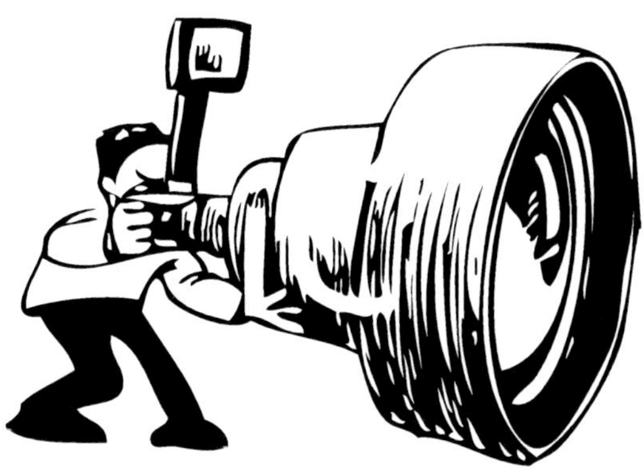

NO UNSAFE PLACES

We're Not Sending You Off to Meth Houses

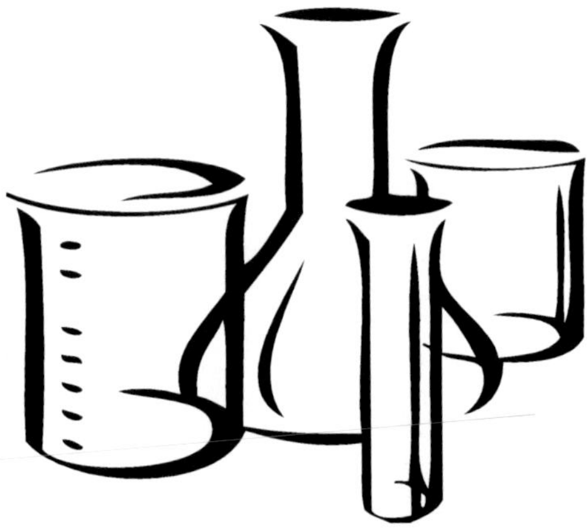

While we love to explore new places, we try to exercise (ugh, bad word) caution and some common sense, like NOT pulling into a driveway or deserted place, especially if we see old pick up trucks and smoke coming out of windows and/or funny smells. We respect "No Trespassing" signs (most of the time) and big, mangy, barking dogs (all of the time).

One afternoon while out on an adventure in the country, we passed a huge junkyard with tons of antique looking pick-ups and vintage, rusty cars. Wow, a virtual gold mine because we LOVE rusty items. Quickly turning the car around Nancy said, *"I'm going to stop and ask this guy if we can take some photos."* We said, *"Are you sure about that because a junkyard reminds us of a junk yard dog and an old song about "Bad Bad LeRoy Brown."* Nancy, really wanting to do this, replied, *"We'll never know unless we ask."*

"*Right*" we agreed, since we didn't plan to get out of the car anyway.

As we were heading down his road we noticed a sign that said, "DON'T BOTHER ME." That was tip-off number one that maybe we shouldn't be there.

Still not deterred, Nancy said she was going to ask anyway and she stopped the car in front of a scary looking building and got out, sort of, with one leg in the car and one out. About that time Big Bubba Leroy Brown stomped out in really dirty overalls and a big snarly look, minus a few teeth. Nothing says IT like gums.

"*Well,*" said Nancy as she jumped back into the car and slammed it into reverse, "*never mind.*"

"*Nice try,*" we muttered.

"PIT STOPS" AND OTHER USELESS INFORMATION

We always have a destination in mind when we start out, but that doesn't mean it's the only place we stop. Far from it. Since we are women, and over 50, we have to make many "pit stops", but Nancy always warns us that once you break the seal, it's a well known fact that you will be constantly making those "pit stops." It's true.

"Pit stops" usually provide us with lots of information (as well as occasional nutritional disasters and drinks). No matter who is working in these culinary-delight establishments, they are usually more than willing to answer:
"Where's your favorite place to go around here?"
"We're a group of crazy, women looking for things to photograph."
"We're photographers and looking for unusual places to photograph … any suggestions?"

We've had a few unprintable suggestions but that's another book. The point is, you have to ask and most will be happy to share.

There are the few people who are leery if they hear the word "professional" (and it's obvious we aren't THAT kind of professional … we'd have to PAY them) so if asked, "Are you professional photographers," we usually just say, "No, we do this for fun, but occasionally earn money to support our photography habit." Well, that is true. I read somewhere that to be considered a "professional photographer" you have to earn half of your living from photography. Well, half of nothing is still nothing. I always excelled in math.

We never know what we are going to find or who we are going to meet or what trouble we might get into or how much weight we are going to gain eating all that tasty, fattening junk food (come on, who hasn't had a Slim Jim??)

If adventure and seeing out-of the-way-places-never-mentioned-in-most-travel-guides, is your calling, grab a friend or a group of friends and get out and go. It's never too late (look at us) to find a new hobby, new friends, new adventures, a business venture, or just plain good old FRIENDSHIP and FUN!!

WHEN IN DOUBT, ASK ... OR NOT

Getting lost while wandering down a country road can be fun if it's not 105 degrees in the shade and you don't need a pit stop. The farther we drove down a country road, the more desperate our needs became. Of course there were NO houses and certainly no gas stations. In the far distance we finally glimpsed a house and it was a unanimous decision to pull in and ask for directions. While there were no barking dogs or Big Bubbas at this place, there was this squarely planted in the front yard:

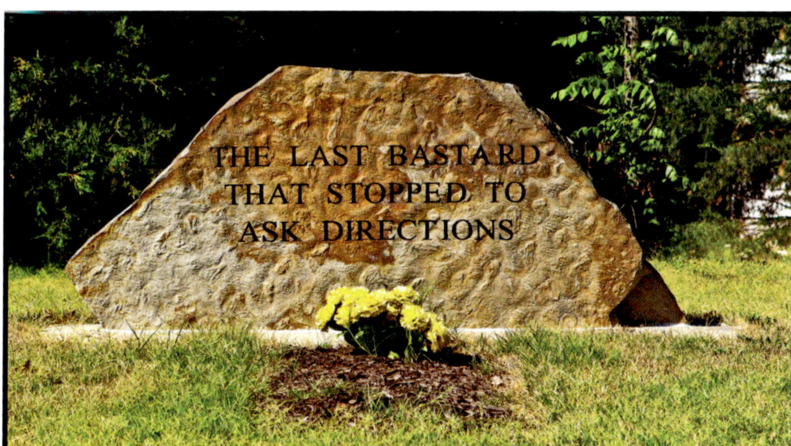

The Last Bastard Who Stopped to Ask Directions.

Some things can't be argued with.

WARNINGS AND OTHER GOOD ADVICE

Taking photographs is addictive; however, not hazardous to your health (wallets yes) unless you step on a patch of ice that's on a hill, as Fearless Angie decided to do on an outing. Not only did she fall really hard, but the lens flew off her camera and slid the rest of the way down the hill. Of course the lens was broken but her camera was fine – probably because she had the strap around her neck! The following week she replaced the lens with another because she was photographing a bachelor/bachelorette party. That lens ended up being knocked (mysteriously) off a table. The good news is it only crushed the protective UV lens and saved the "real" one; however, now there are thousands of pieces of itsy bitsy teeny tiny glass shards and it had to be sent off for cleaning! And so it goes.

Nevertheless, since the rest of the world seems to be hung up on posting WARNINGS everywhere (did you ever read the side of a ladder?), we thought we should, too.

- Don't crawl under farm fences, no matter how tempting it is to get "up close and personal" with that cute cow or sheep. It's private property and there may be an unhappy bull looking for a mate; or an owner preparing to use you for target practice. Then, there are those electrified fences.

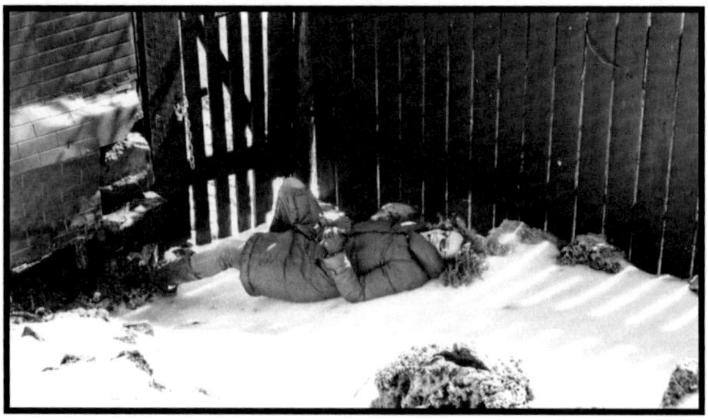

Angie Lying Down on the Job.

- Never take a child's photograph without permission of the parent and certainly don't post it on the internet.

- Keep your safety in mind. We have decided that if we are in an area that is perhaps a little deserted, two of us shoot while the other keeps an eye on our surroundings. It's so easy to get totally engrossed in what you are shooting that you stop paying attention to what's going on around you.

WHAT ABOUT SHOOTING PEOPLE ON THE STREET? (We're talking CAMERA shooting.)

Some Thoughts on Street Photography by Jeff Hirsch

In loose terms, 'street photography' is concerned with subjects in candid situations within public places. It doesn't have to be in an urban environment or even occur on a paved street. 'Street' simply refers to a place where human activity can be seen, a place to observe and capture social interaction. It's a form of photography that puts the shooter in direct (and sometimes indirect) contact with complete strangers in a public place, and as such it can be very intimidating to novice and even experienced photographers as they encounter both the social and legal implications of this style of shooting.

The two most common questions I get have to do with how to get comfortable shooting strangers in public situations and what one's legal rights are as a photographer. I will address the legal issues first since they are more cut and dried. The rest are more a matter of opinion and personal style.

JEFF HIRSCH

PART I: Legal Considerations for Street Photographers

Let me start with the following (legally required) disclaimer:

Disclaimer: This information does not constitute legal advice, nor does it establish an attorney-client relationship. The information contained herein is no substitute for legal advice from an attorney licensed in your state and may or may not be applicable to your specific situation. You are strongly encouraged to consult with local counsel to discuss your individual circumstances.

The short version is that I am not a lawyer and nothing I say here should be construed as legal advice.

Let's start with the basics...

Q: Do I need a model release to publish images with street photography subjects?
A: No, not unless you will be using their image in a commercial context.

Q: Can I sell my street photos or publish them in a book without a model release?
A: Yes, you can still sell your images as prints or in books. What you can't do is use one of the images in a commercial advertisement where your subject could be construed as promoting or advocating a particular product or service. This is what is meant by "commercial usage." In that case, you'd need a model release.

Q: What are the restrictions regarding shooting a person in public view?
A: As long as you are shooting from public ground, you can photograph whatever and whoever you wish; including persons situated on private property but within public view, such as a through a shop-window, cafe or other similar situation. The same goes for private property, buildings, etc. If you are on public ground, you may legally photograph private property

visible from where you stand or sit. In the United States, you do not need to obtain parental consent to photograph children on or visible from public property.

Q: Really?
A: Yes, really! But use your common sense. There are some limits on what you are allowed to shoot – socially, ethically and legally.

Where there are limits, they are related to a person's "reasonable expectation of privacy". People have a reasonable expectation of privacy in their bedrooms and bathrooms, at the doctor's office, in store changing rooms, and in other similar sensitive areas of society. So, if you go pointing your camera in somebody's bedroom or bathroom window, you are both ethically and legally on thin ice.

Sure, it's legal for you to follow women and children through the public streets of your city in an effort to capture a nice image, but you are likely to be perceived as a creeper or lurker if you do so in a threatening or sneaky manner. Laws and social customs vary by country and even by state, so be sure you know what is appropriate for your locality when shooting.

Q: Are there limitations on what gear I can set up in a public location?
A: If your tripod and lighting kit has the potential to disrupt the general flow of traffic, interfere with official activities like police, fire, and maintenance crews, or cause some sort of safety hazard, you may need a permit to shoot with your gear in that location. This is particularly true of crowded and busy places like airports, train stations, etc.

For example, you can shoot hand-held without a permit at Grand Central Terminal in NYC. But as soon as you put down a tripod, the police and security officers will approach you and ask for your shooting permit. (Hint: if you don't have one in advance, you can usually go to the station-master's office and get one on the spot.)

Q: What about public spaces likes malls, stadiums, theaters, etc?
A: Public spaces are not always public property. Most malls, stadia, and performance venues are privately owned and considered private property. They may, therefore, set limits on photography taken within their bounds. If the owner or one of their agents (security guard, employee, etc.) asks you to stop shooting or to leave the premises, you are legally required to comply with that request.

Q: What about government facilities like courthouses, statehouses, and military installations?
A: Despite the heightened scrutiny that photographers are getting in the "post 9/11" world, most (non-military) government buildings are fair game for photographers. A 2010 federal court ruling has codified the right of photographers to shoot the outside of any and all federal buildings nationwide. In the settlement, approved by a federal judge in Manhattan, the government acknowledged that there are no federal laws or regulations that prohibit photography outside federal buildings. It agreed to provide federal officers written instructions emphasizing the public's right to photograph and record outside federal buildings.

Despite the ruling and the distribution of written instructions describing the ruling, many law officers continue to believe the practice is illegal. So, you may still find yourself getting questioned by well intentioned, but otherwise misinformed members of law enforcement.

It's important to note here that commanders of military installations can prohibit photographs of specific areas when they deem it necessary to protect national security. The U.S. Department of Energy can also prohibit photography of designated nuclear facilities although the publicly visible areas of nuclear facilities are usually not designated as such.

My suggestion for all american photographers is that you download and print out a copy of this listing of Photographer's Rights so you can present it to any public or private agent who questions you while you are doing street shooting. It's a good primer on the law and how to react if stopped.

http://www.krages.com/ThePhotographersRight.pdf

Q: Am I allowed to photograph the police? What about a crime or accident scene?
A: Contrary to popular belief, you are within your rights to photograph any of the following so long as you are shooting from a public place and are not interfering with an officer doing his or her job. This includes:

accident, crime, and fire scenes
bridges, tunnels, and other infrastructure
residential and commercial buildings
industrial facilities and public utilities
transportation hubs like airports, train stations, bus stations, subway stations
criminal activities
law enforcement officers, firemen, paramedics, and other rescue personnel.

Q: Am I required to surrender or erase my images if asked to do so by a security guard or other agent?
A: No, you are not. Without a court order, private parties have no right to confiscate your film or digital image. Taking your film directly or indirectly by threat of force or by threatening to call a law enforcement agency can be considered the criminal offense of theft or coercion. Neither private citizens nor law enforcement officials have the authority or right to require that you delete your photographs or relinquish your equipment

(including your film or memory cards) except when acting in accordance with a court order or in conducting of a lawful arrest.

Q: What do I do if confronted during a shoot by police, security, or a private citizen?
A: First off... be calm, be respectful, and be prepared to explain yourself if necessary to defuse the situation.

While there are some people who will hassle photographers for no good reason at all, try to understand that most police and security personnel are probably coming from a place of fear, defensiveness, or concern for public safety. Calmly and honestly explain to those who ask what or why you are shooting that you are a professional photographer, a photographer taking part in a photo walk, or a photography student completing an assignment. Any one of these explanations is very likely to defuse the situation.

If you are told that your activity or your gear is prohibited, you may respectfully ask for clarification as to the relevant policy, regulation, or statute and if it applies to you. In general, private citizens may not detain you unless they have witnessed a felony being committed. Law enforcement officials may detain you only if they have reasonable suspicion of your involvement in criminal activity.

Concerned parties like police and security officers are within their rights to inquire briefly about your activities, but they are not allowed to badger, harass, or detain you. Asking "am I free to go?" is often a good approach when the questions go on longer than you are comfortable with. Most private and public safety officers will understand that short of arresting you, they can't detain you for more than a few minutes of questioning.

JEFF HIRSCH

PART II: Shooting Strangers in Public Places

Now that we've gotten all that legal mumbo-jumbo out of the way, we can address the actual art and practice of street shooting.

Technical Considerations:

Street photography is generally a fast moving activity even if you are standing completely still. The situations unfolding in front of your camera happen in a split second and are gone, sometimes never to be seen again. If you want to get the shot, you and your gear need to be ready to capture the decisive moment the split-second it occurs.

As far as your camera is concerned, you should consider shooting in shutter priority mode and keeping your shutter speed at 1/250 of a second or faster. This ensures that your subject will be frozen in time and minimizes any motion blur. In order to get a shutter speed this fast, you may need to push your ISO to 1600 or higher, even in broad daylight. Many "pixel peepers" are overly concerned with noise in their images and will shoot at the lowest possible ISO in every situation. And while this may minimize the noise in their shots, it more often than not reduces shutter speed to the point where the image may be soft or even blurred. As the great photographer Jay Maisel is fond of saying "I am more interested in picture quality than pixel quality." What good is a noise-free image if the subject itself is still blurry?

If you are shooting at 1/250th of a second, you might also need to push your ISO up if you find your aperture is getting too wide and your depth of field has gotten too shallow. There's nothing worse than getting a perfectly focused picture of the background and not the subject you had intended. Try to shoot with enough depth to capture your subject.

TIP: Consider using the "back-button focus" feature of your camera (if it has one). This allows you to set and lock the focus with one button (usually on the back of your camera) and then release the shutter with the normal trigger button at the precise moment you are ready. Shooting in this fashion can help you avoid refocusing when it isn't necessary and makes it possible to get some of those split-second images that would have been lost if the camera was busy seeking focus at the critical moment. Back-button focus takes a little getting used to, but I find that once a photographer gets comfortable shooting this way, they never return to a single focus-meter-shutter release method.

TIP: In general, know your camera and know it well. You don't want to be fiddling with settings while a wonderful moment is happening right in front of you. Be prepared to compose and shoot as quickly as possible. This means reading your manual (yes, really!) and it means practicing with your camera in different lighting environments until it becomes second nature and you don't even need to think about it.

Mental Considerations:

Almost everything else about street photography is mental and emotional. You need to get your head and heart and eyes in the right place to see and capture the moments as they are happening in front of you.

Ideally, you want to be in a receptive mind-frame and open to whatever possibilities unfold. Street photography is about taking what comes at you in life and much less about trying to pose or control the subject. (Street portraits are another genre almost entirely and we won't address them here.)

JEFF HIRSCH

TIP: Try to go out shooting without any preconceptions or expectations. Instead, try to be open and receptive to what the world brings into your frame. Your images will be much more genuine this way. Trying to plan a street shoot is a quick route to boring and predictable photographs. The world is a random and strange place. Use that fact to your advantage!

A simple exercise for new street shooters is to set yourself up across from or in front of an interesting background. It could be a graffiti covered wall, a large print advertisement, a series of store fronts, or anything else you think makes for a good backdrop. Then wait for subjects to walk into your frame where they are juxtaposed with the background. When you spot a moment that appeals to you, take the shot.

TIP: Don't stop shooting after the first keeper! Keep your eye on the subject and keep shooting until the you have exhausted all the possibilities in the scene. While you were busy looking down at the first good shot you took, another dozen good shots may have happened without you even noticing. Keep shooting! Wonderful and amazing surprises can and will happen long after you've gotten the "money" shot.

The next consideration is where to place yourself for shooting. Shooters who are shy or uncomfortable interacting with strangers will invariably set up across the street from what they are shooting and capture images from that safe distance using a long zoom lens.

While this method does prevent you from ever having to make contact with your subject, it also removes you completely from the scene itself and makes it much harder to capture a truly up-close and personal image. Closer almost always equals better in street photography.

A better approach is to shoot your subjects directly and in close proximity – not from a great distance. Put a wide angle lens on your camera and learn to get comfortable being much closer to the people and scenes you are shooting. Your photographs will be much more compelling if you make this one basic choice.

TIP: Don't be furtive, sneaky, or try to hide what you are doing. People become more suspicious if you try to take pictures sneakily or if you look nervous. If you act as though you're doing your job and you project a more comfortable and confident body language, then you're much less likely to get hassled.

Be obvious and overt about what you are doing. If you get "busted" by somebody who spots you shooting them, don't skulk away or pretend you weren't aiming at them. Just smile at them! A sheepish "yeah, you caught me" grin goes a long way with most people. My basic mindset is to act like a "happy idiot" when I get guff from a subject. Most people don't get too upset with me when I act this way.

Here's a good example: I was shooting in a New York subway station earlier this year just as a train pulled in. I spotted a beautiful young woman sitting in one of the window seats and put my camera to my eye to get a shot. As I pulled the trigger on the first shot, she spotted me and had a look on her face that was a mixture of anger and fear. "Who is this guy and why is he pointing a camera at me?" I knew I had a split-second to change the tenor of the interaction, so I immediately smiled a big broad smile back at her, shrugged my shoulders, and flashed her the peace sign. Her demeanor changed in an instant and she responded by giving me a million-watt smile I never would have captured if I hadn't actually interacted with her when she busted me. Getting busted isn't the end of the world, sometimes it's the beginning of a whole new interaction with your subject.

TIP: If somebody really doesn't want their picture taken, my advice is to not take their picture. Sounds simple, right? Yet I find that so many photographers get insulted or offended at such a suggestion. "How dare you tell me I can't shoot somebody in public?!", they cry. But the truth is, do you really need that particular shot? Is it really worth it to make somebody unhappy this way? Will it really be the difference between a successful and a failed shoot? Probably not. Most of the time you just end up pissing people off and giving photographers a bad reputation as being rude and invasive. As Jay Maisel says "I don't want to ruin somebody's day." If you are getting clear signs that your subject is not happy being shot, use your best judgement and err on the side of caution.

With all of that being said, there are some ways to hide in plain sight, or at the least minimize your profile so people don't notice you as readily. You are trying to be unobtrusive not invisible. The following series of tips can help reduce the amount of attention you call to yourself in a street shooting environment.

TIP: Dress casually and avoid looking like a photographer if at all possible. Leave that fancy photo vest at home and wear dark colored clothing unless it would make you stick out in a crowd. Bright saturated colors will draw people's attention directly to you. The idea is to blend in.

TIP: If you are shooting in broad daylight, find a place in the shade or the shadows to stand or sit. On a bright day, you will be almost unseen if you are standing in the shadows and your subject is in the light – even on a busy street.

TIP: Consider what camera, lens, and even lens hood you are shooting with. Big dSLR rigs with jumbo zoom lenses and even longer lens hoods can be very intimidating to your subject. Most people don't like the feeling of having a bazooka pointed at them. If you have a smaller camera (micro 4/3 or the like) you might take that instead of your big gun as you will look much more like a "normal person" and not a photographer.

Whenever possible, only bring the equipment you need. Extra

batteries, lots of extra memory cards and maybe an extra lens if you absolutely must have it. The less you look like a photographer, the better the pictures you will get. So, avoid overly large camera bags. If you must bring extra gear, consider a fanny pack or courier bag which look much less like camera bags.

TIP: Mingle with the crowd. At first they will probably stare at you, but in a short time, they will lose interest and forget about you. That's when you can really get some candid moments.The key ingredient to good photography is time. Be patient and stick it out. Don't leave just because you get a little uncomfortable. Don't leave after the first couple of decent shots. You never know what is waiting for you around the next corner.

TIP: ALWAYS carry your camera with you. If you are serious about street photography, you need to have your camera with you at all times. Get used to carrying it around. Get comfortable pulling it out when you see a moment worth capturing. As the great Wayne Gretzky used to say "You miss 100% of the shots you don't take."

TIP: Don't be afraid to talk to your subjects. Ask them if you can take their picture. Ask them to move into better light if that's what you really want for your shot. Purist street shooters may scoff at this idea, as the photo becomes more like a street portrait, but most of us aren't bound by such narrow restrictions on street shooting. Most photographers will benefit greatly from actually talking to and with their subjects. In fact, the longer you talk to somebody and get comfortable with them before taking their picture, the more likely you are to get an honest and connected photo of them. Start simple – ask their name, where they are from, what their passions are in life. Find out what makes them tick and use it to elicit a good expression from them when you do get around to shooting. If the situation permits, turn the camera around and show them

JEFF HIRSCH

some of the better images as you shoot. Very often the next shots you take will be even better because they have seen what you are doing and will adjust accordingly. Sometimes, they just relax and smile more naturally. (And we all know how tough it is to get a natural smile out of people!)

This means getting over your fear of talking to strangers. Sometimes, you just have to take a big gulp, walk up to a person and introduce yourself and your intentions. The more you practice this, the easier it gets. I promise.

Locations for Street Photography:

Lastly, I want to leave you with a few ideas about where to shoot.

For me, the more crowded the environment, the better. There are more little moments unfolding in front of you and you are more likely to blend into a busy crowd. Any direction you point your camera is likely to have something interesting going on.

For that reason I love farmers markets, parades, zoos, parks, 4th of July celebrations, state fairs, sports rallies, Mardi Gras, art or street fairs, and just about any other place where people congregate in large groups.

In the metro St. Louis area, one of my all time favorite places for street photography is the Soulard Farmer's Market on a Saturday morning. The place is positively teeming with shoppers and vendors and it's easy to blend in with the bustling crowd.

Octoberfest and Fair St. Louis also offer some really great street shooting situations.

Another favorite place to shoot is in and around the stadium before or after a Cardinals baseball game. Any place there are swarms of people, there will be good street shooting.

External Resources and References:

http://erickimphotography.com/blog/start-here/

http://everydayaperture.com/law/

http://www.clickinmoms.com/blog/street-photography-and-the-law-7-things-you-need-to-know/

http://www.digitalcameraworld.com/2010/03/26/21-street-photography-tips-from-the-professionals/

http://www.nyclu.org/news/nyclu-settlement-ends-restriction-photography-outside-federal-courthouses

http://www.murthalawfirm.com/photographers-rights-affirmed-ny-arrest-simply-pictures-public-federal-buildings

http://www.krages.com/phoright.htm

Missouri Destinations

All Within 150 Miles of Downtown St. Louis

THREE
Reed Spring Mill
Centerville, Missouri

This place is so gorgeous it's well worth the drive – any time of the year. Plus, it's *superbly* **scenic** down Highway 21 and there are LOTS of photo ops along the way. Here's some history about the mill if you are interested:

In 1881, Nathaniel Scott built the dam and grist mill to grind the corn into meal and wheat into flour. Later, a saw mill was erected supplying much needed lumber to early settlers to build their homes. In or around 1915, a Dr. Shy had the idea of generating electricity from its water power, so they took off the overshot wheel, installed a turbine and ran electric lines into Centerville. Though the lights were bright at the mill, but dim in town, this supplied the towns' electricity until 1929.

Although privately owned, this incredibly picturesque **mill**, with a working **waterwheel**, and of course the **spring** – is fully visible from the road. There is also an **old house** to the left (great **old window** and **texture** shots) and the **Black River** runs along the **gravel road**.

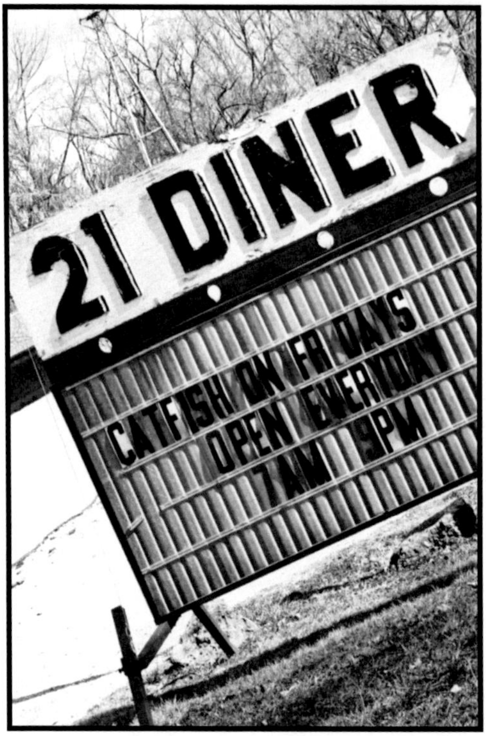

Note: There are a couple of friendly dogs that might greet you. The owner lives in the house to the right as you are facing the actual Mill. We didn't ask to shoot because Nancy, on a previous trip, spoke with the owner. I think it's up to you to ask or not. The dogs might ask for a tip.

Approximate Mileage from Downtown St. Louis: 115 miles

Directions: Take 40/64 West from St. Louis to 270 South (I think the exit also says "Memphis" at this particular spot). Take 270 South to Tesson Ferry and head west. Tesson Ferry is also known as 21. Take 21 through Caledonia, Ironton, past entrance to Johnson's Shut-Ins and keep on driving! Make sure you stay on 21 as the road twists and turns a bit. When you get into Centerville, follow 21 until you see a little diner, 21 Diner, and it will be on your right. Go past the diner (less than l/2 mile) and go west or left on Pine Street. It's a one-lane gravel road and it's only about a tenth of a mile and the Mill is on your right. You can't miss it!

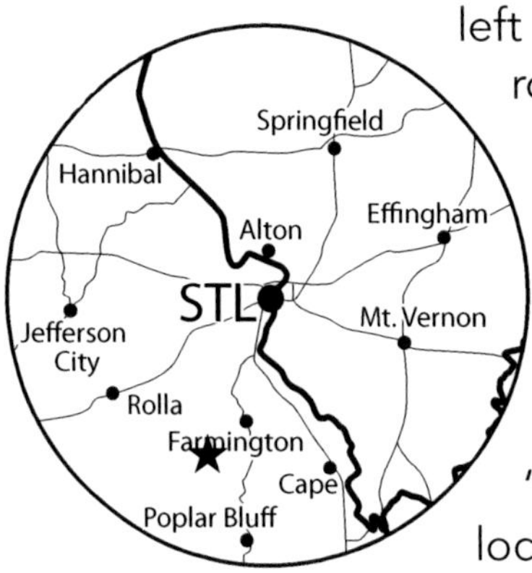

Food: We stopped in the little town of Centerville to do what else … get drinks and make the normal "pit stop." It was a long drive. The local place is called 21 Diner and besides drinks, they had some sandwiches.

Handicap Accessibility: Excellent. You can see everything from the car.

Celebrity Alert: In the Diner they have a picture of the Mountain Lion that was captured in early 2012. Not to scare you or anything, but this is the part of the country where he was discovered. Yikes!

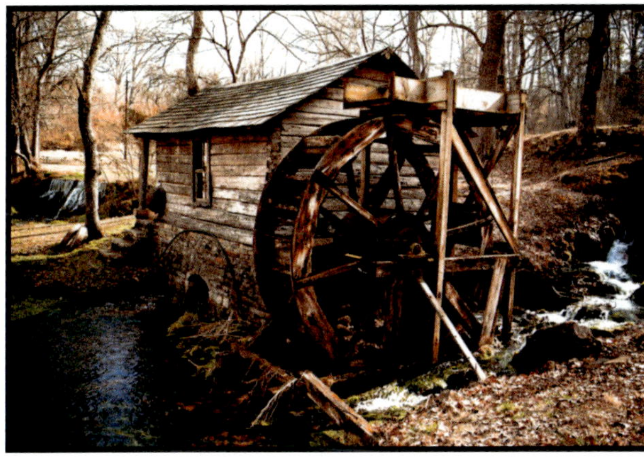

Reed Mill

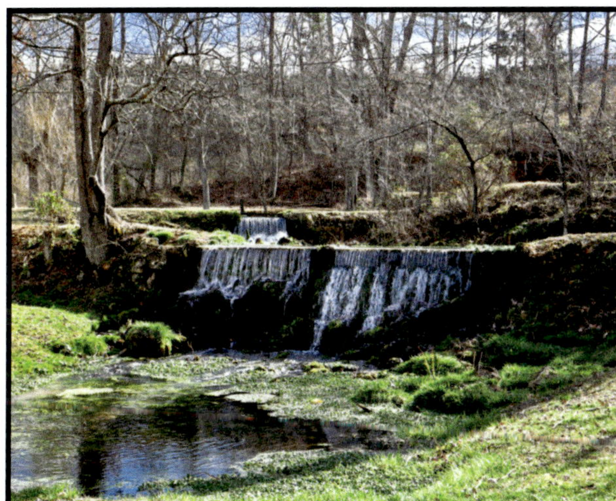

Springs at Reed Mill

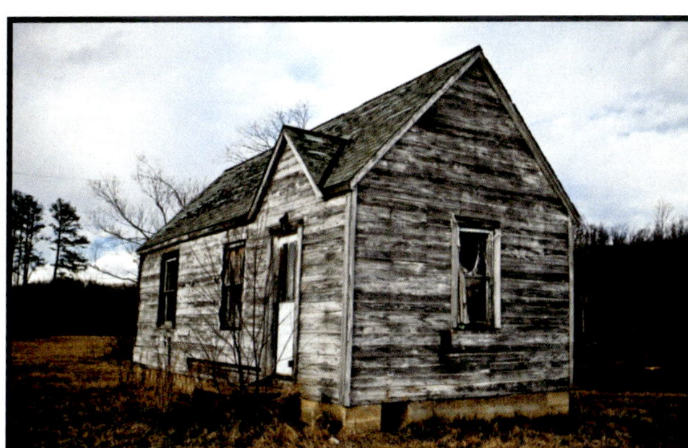

Old Deserted House on 21

FOUR
Callaway Fork Road
New Melle, Missouri

A road for a destination? Really? Honest, this is the best kept secret for miles around and it's on the way to New Melle, Missouri. You will think you're going down someone's driveway to their hidden estate, but it's really a winding **country road**, (and public since it is maintained by St. Charles County) … gravel and all. The road is narrow so you will have to pull over to let cars pass from the other side. However, they are few and far between. There is plenty of room to pull off to park when you decide to stop and haul out your cameras or simply gawk at the beauty.

This road is very **scenic** because it goes down between the hills and you will be crossing lots of **creeks**. The creeks are very natural but during a drought, like the Summer of 2012, you will see very little water. During normal times of the year we have always seen water flowing. A creek runs along side the road with lots of **natural rock formations** and various levels of rocks which make the water gurgle and bubble as it flows downstream.

You can take a "real" car down this road but if you have access to an SUV we highly recommend it since they tend to sit higher than a "real" car. As I said, this IS a **gravel road** and you will be crossing creeks on **low water concrete slab bridges** so it's not something we wanted to do in our BMW convertible. Yeah, right.

The land on either side of the road is private property so it's not advisable to go wandering off into the woods over hill and dale unless you loved the movie "Deliverance." Seriously, this area is perfectly safe and I used to take my children there when they were little guys to play in the creeks. Just respect others' property. Did I really have to say that?

Nevertheless, besides the **creeks** along this road you will see **horses** in a pasture, a **deserted farm house** and a **barn** (again, we have never ventured into these because there are sounds of those dueling banjos), **farm fields** with **rock bluffs**, **wildlife**, etc. AND, the road is passable, except during heavy rains. We have never had the nerve to drive into a creek on one of those low water concrete slab bridges with water swirling, who knows how deep. Remember hearing commercials during flood season, "Turn Around. Don't Drown?" They mean it and so do we!

We visited Callaway Fork Road this year, in the late summer and again in mid-October. The **fall colors** were spectacular. Fall always wins out in our book! The naturally **curvy winding country road** also lends itself to Photo Ops, particularly with the trees "on fire" this year.

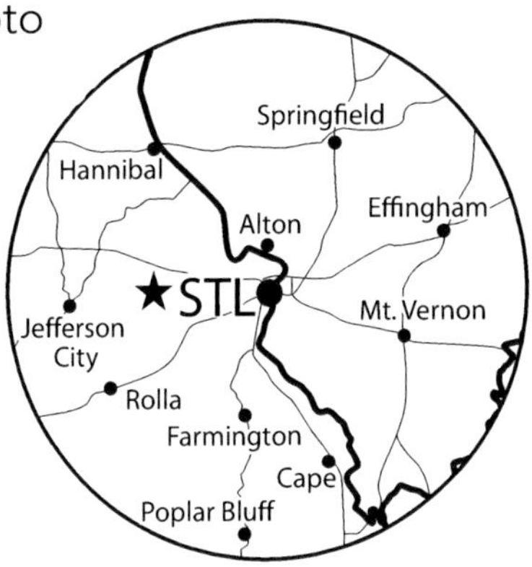

Approximate miles from Downtown St. Louis: 42 miles

Directions: Callaway Fork Road is off Highway D that goes into New Melle. But for the bigger picture …

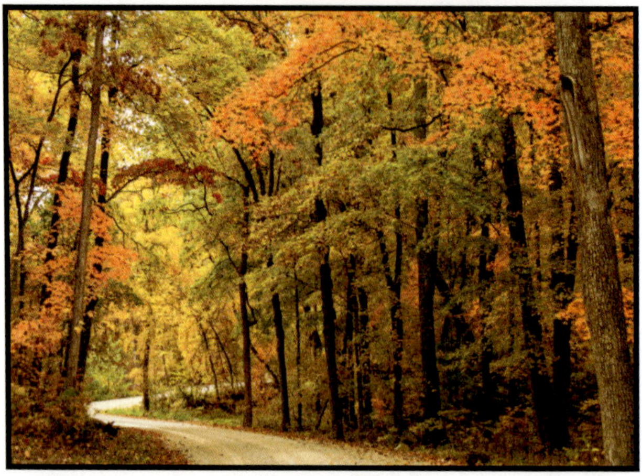

Callaway Fork Road

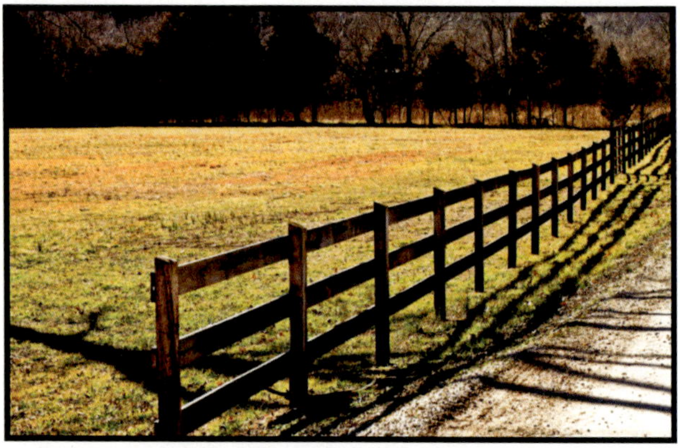

Scenic Field on Callaway Fork Road

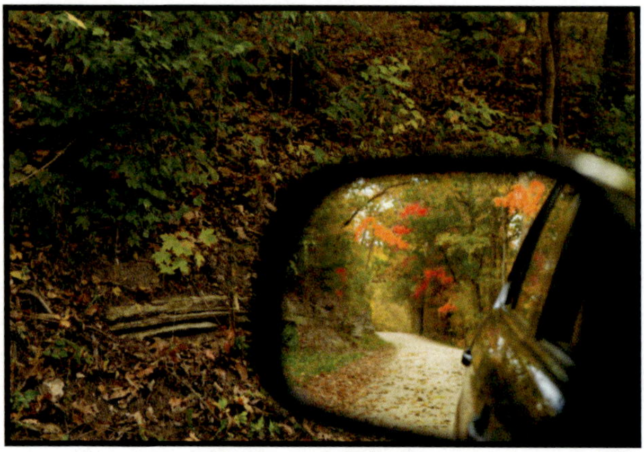

View From Behind

take 40/64 West across the Missouri River (just past Chesterfield Valley). Exit at Highway 94 and go left or south. You will be crossing back over 40/64 and at the next stoplight you will go right or west on Highway D. Follow Highway D for about 5 miles to the first stop sign, which will be at the intersection of D and DD. There is also a gas station and mini-mart. Stay on Highway D for approximately 3 more miles. You will see a sign on your left, for Callaway Farms Subdivision and Callaway Fork Road. Make a left. THE TRICK is to not go into the subdivision, which veers off to the right. Instead, stay straight and you should see a sign that says "Callaway Fork Road." The pavement only lasts for a couple of seconds and then you will be on the Callaway Fork Road. Gravel Roads – here you come!

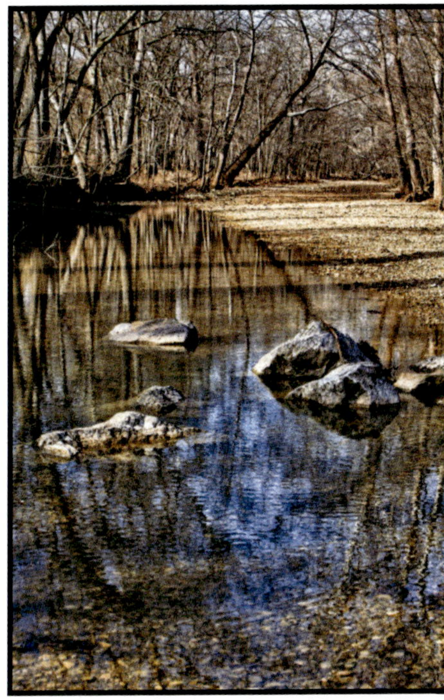

A Creek on Callaway Fork Road During Winter

Another hint: Callaway Fork Road goes all the way through to Highway F, ONLY IF ITS NOT RAINING. Remember what we told you about those concrete slab "bridges"? Do not cross over them if we've been having heavy rains!!

Food: You are in the heart of wine country. Follow the directions above and you will end up on Highway F, which takes you to wineries. We will list the wineries in Chapter Eleven, Femme Osage.

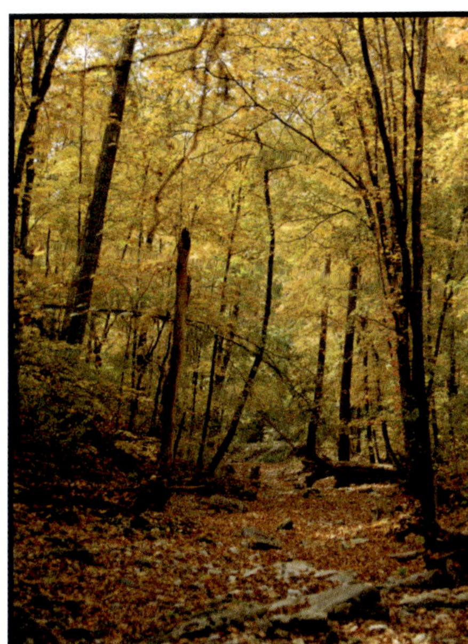

Dry Creek Bed Along Callaway Fork Road

Handicap Accessible: Very good since the road is flat. Then, walk and take those photographs.

FIVE
Missouri Mines State Historic Site and St. Joe State Park
Park Hills, Missouri

Photo Op #1
Missouri Mines State Historic Site

*This is an absolute treasure of history, **old industrial buildings** with lots of **rust**, **broken windows**, **gears**, **equipment**, and **mine machinery**.*

*The area was once home to the largest **lead mine** in Missouri and also called the Old Lead Belt area. The actual mine was called the St. Joseph Lead Company. In 1980 the 25-acre mine-mill was designated as a Missouri Mines State historic site and it is a great **industrial site**.*

When you first spot the buildings it can appear as if they are deserted. Never fear! There is a large parking lot behind the buildings and on the day we were there, the place was empty except for a park ranger. You can walk around various areas, and all are clearly marked. The ranger gave us a tour but you can't actually go inside any of the buildings for safety reasons; however, there are plenty of **windows** and big, **old doors**

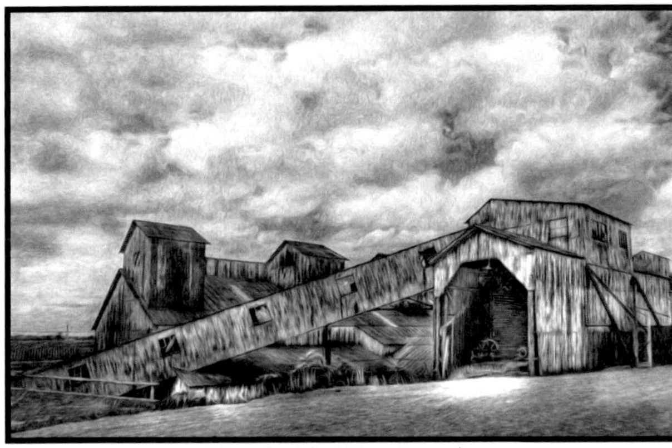

View Inside Mine Complex

where you may stand and take photographs. Inside the Main Building is a **museum** but we just ran out of time. There wasn't a charge for entering at the time we were there. They just ask for a donation, which seemed more than fair to us for all the great photographs we took.

Approximate miles from Downtown St. Louis: 70 miles

Directions: Take Highway 55 South to Highway 67 South. Go approximately 30 miles. Take the Park Hills Exit 32, turn right, go one mile & turn right on Business 32. Your destination is 0.2 miles past Clemons Road. The Mine sits on your left so you actually pass it first and then enter. The address is 4000 State Highway 32, Park Hills, MO 63601 and the phone number is 573-431-6226.

Food: Across the highway from the Mine is a little town called Park Hills. Our favorite spot for lunch is the Main Street Grill. Yummy food and homemade desserts. The **town** is **old** and has some interesting **old buildings**.

Handicap Accessibility: Very good and perfectly flat, but paved with small gravel so it could be a problem for a wheelchair.

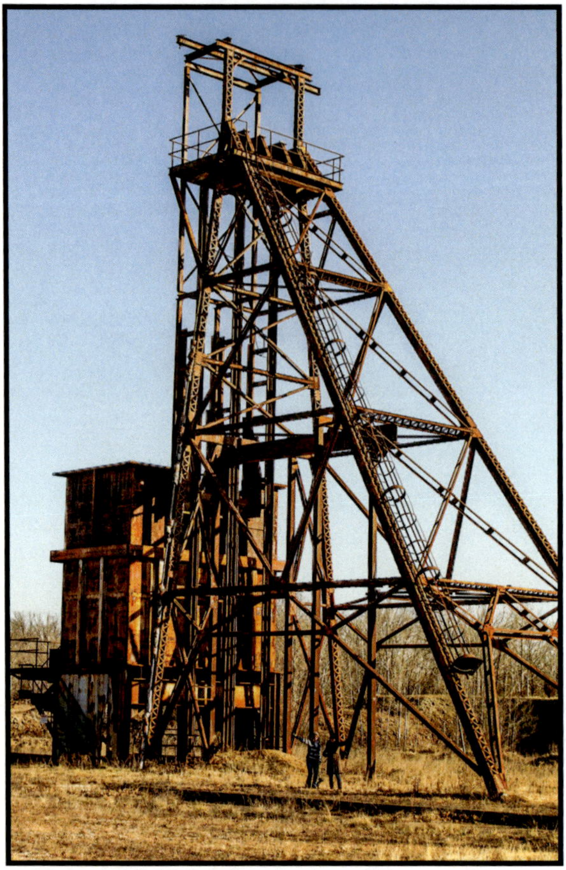

Missouri Eiffel Tower. See Angie and Nancy at Bottom.

Photo Op #2 St. Joe State Park and "The Missouri Eiffel Tower"

This state park is behind the mine complex, but you will need to drive to it.

In the middle of the park, not obvious until you pass it, is a huge structure that we called the **Missouri Eiffel Tower**. It's not the official name, of course, but we thought it fit. It's on a much smaller scale than the real Eiffel Tower, of course, and there are no cute little café tables and handsome waiters with wine bottles hovering over you whispering sweet little French ditties in your ear. This structure covers an old mine and served as a place where the lead ore was loaded into rail cars.

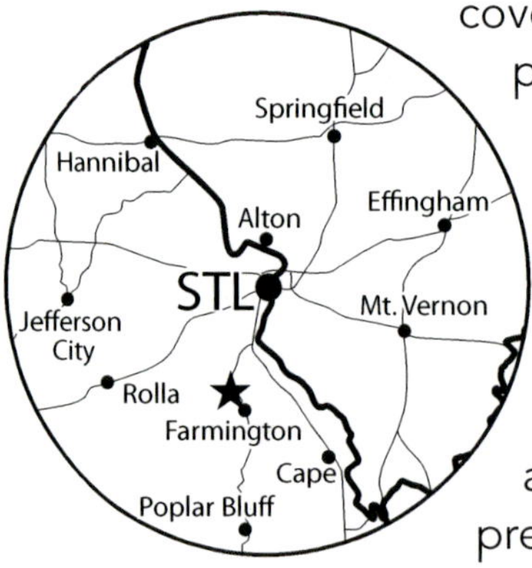

Besides being an interesting **structure**, it was loaded with **rust** – our personal favorite. Don't worry, you aren't going to fall into any old mines. The Park has them pretty well covered. There were a couple of kids there (anyone under 30 is a kid to us) and they were climbing on the actual structure. We admit it did look tempting, and as we were leaving, a ranger was headed in that direction to slap some hurt on someone. It wasn't us!

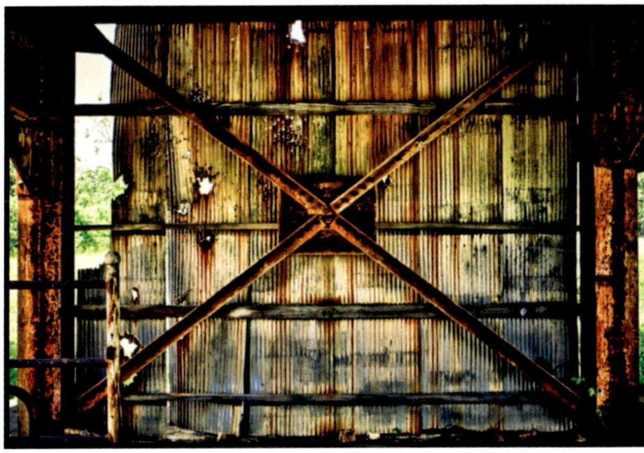

Good Rust Inside the Eiffel Tower

Directions: Take Pimville Road straight to the Missouri Eiffel Tower. You will pass the office entrance on the left, the Blankshire Trail head on your right, and then the road makes a sharp left. Park your car right in front of the only path. This will take you to the tower. It's a short walk (maybe a

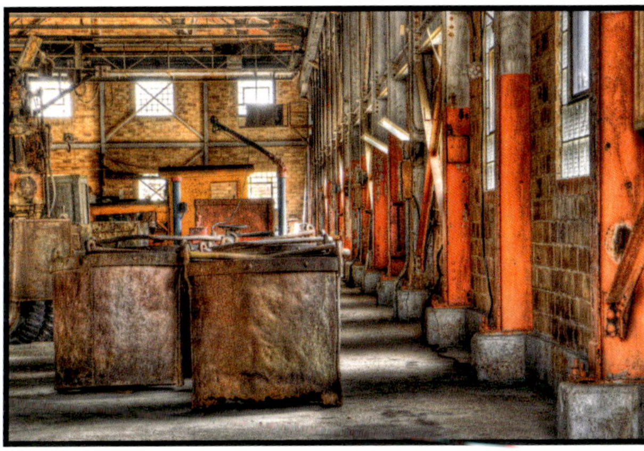

Inside the Missouri Mine Building

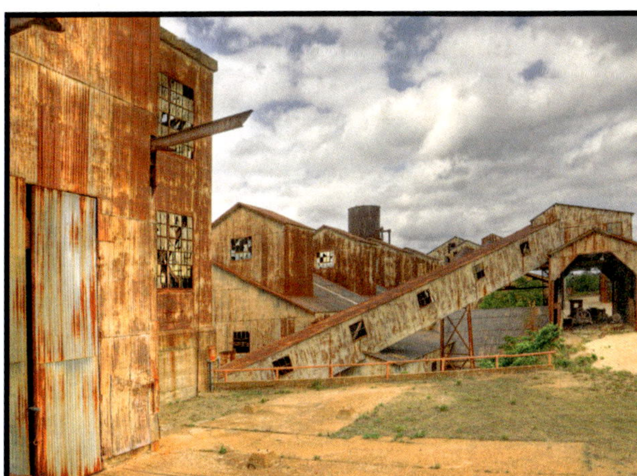

View Inside the Mine Complex

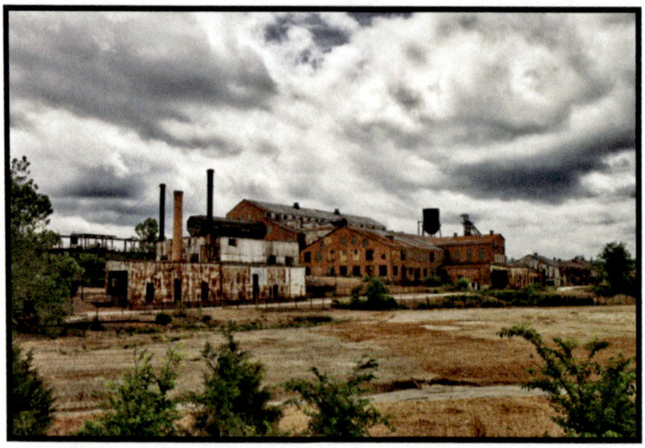

St. Joe Mine Company Photographed from Road.

block) and the ground is flat. You can't miss it.

Photo Op #3 and #4 St. Joe State Park

This park also has a couple of other fun things to photograph; one being a really large, flat, dusty area dedicated to off road vehicles. There were a lot of people in fancy, **bright colored** outfits and helmets speeding around so a chance for some good **action shots**.

The other Op being a nice lake with a sandy beach, picnic areas, and of course the natural beauty of the park itself.

Approximate miles from Downtown St. Louis: 79. This Park is behind the mine complex and while you have to drive, it's only another mile or so.

Directions: 2800 Pimville Road, Park Hills, MO 63601. Go past the Mine entrance (stay on Mo-32W) and then turn left onto Pimville Road. Turn left at office entrance on your left and follow this road to the ORV Riding Area and Lake.

Food: Town of Park Hills listed above.

Handicap Accessibility: We would say Very Good because the ORV area has a huge parking lot (small gravel) but flat and you can park right by one of the courses. The lake with the sandy beach also has a paved parking lot and it's a short walk to the beach.

SIX

Black Madonna Shrine and Grottos

Eureka, Missouri

This little gem is located outside Eureka, Missouri. It's a nice change of pace for those needing serenity, as well as **unusual scenics**. The Black Madonna Shrine offers many **mosaics** and **multi-colored rock sculptures**. The grottos, which are constructed of Missouri tiff rock, are set back into the hills. In the grottos you will find several places to sit and just "be." This site is maintained by the Franciscan Missionary Brothers and the origins of this religious setting trace back to 1927. Up on the hill from the Grottos (and next to the parking lot) is the open-air **Chapel** of the Hills. This building does have a roof; it's just the sides that are open. There is a lovely **altar** and, of course, the lighting is great.

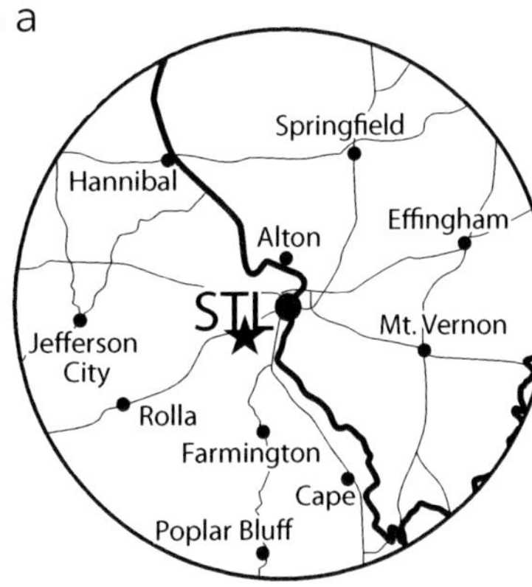

We also have to mention that "Black Madonna" is a nickname (not given by us). It refers to skin tones in a centuries old painting called "Our Lady of Czestochowa – The Miraculous Image," which is a

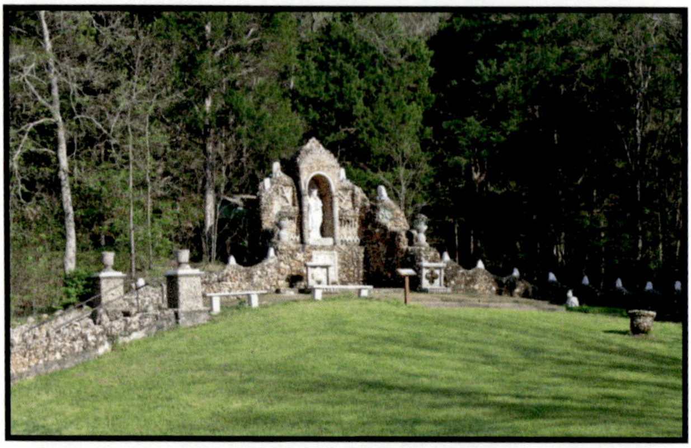

One of the Hand Built Grottos

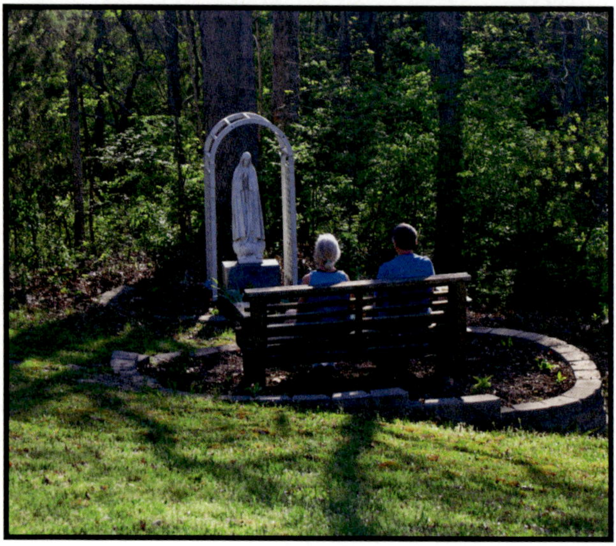

A Restful Spot

portrait of Mary and Jesus.

For more history, visit this website www.franciscan-caring.org/black-madonnashri.html

Approximate miles from Downtown St. Louis: 34 miles

Directions: Take Interstate 44 to the Eureka exit. Turn south onto Highway 109 and drive to Highway FF. Turn right onto FF and drive to Highway F. Turn left onto F, then drive to St. Joseph's Road. There you will make a right. The entrance to the Black Madonna Shrine and Grottos will be on your left.

Food: There is nothing available, except "food for the spirit."

Handicap Accessibility: Fairly decent. A wheelchair can be taken to the Chapel, which is next to the parking lot, and there you will have a great view of the Shrine and Grottos. However, the rest is pretty hilly, but walkable.

SEVEN
Riverside Wildlife Ranch, a.k.a. The Reptile Ranch
Stanton, Missouri

You will be heading to Stanton, Missouri and this place is really weird. We were fascinated, in a sick kind of way. The sign out front says, "Jewelry, Reptiles, Gifts." Hey, jewelry always gets my attention. At least it *didn't* say "Guns, Ammo, Bait and Gifts" ... so in we went.

The "Gift Store" was full of strange "memorabilia" like **reptile** teeth and **snake skins** – need I say more? We presumed the man in the back was the owner and while he didn't look like Crocodile Dundee, he did have on a similar hat. He was feeding a baby skunk (in case you don't know – we didn't – they don't have their "stinker" in gear at this young age.) Who wouldn't fall for a baby skunk?

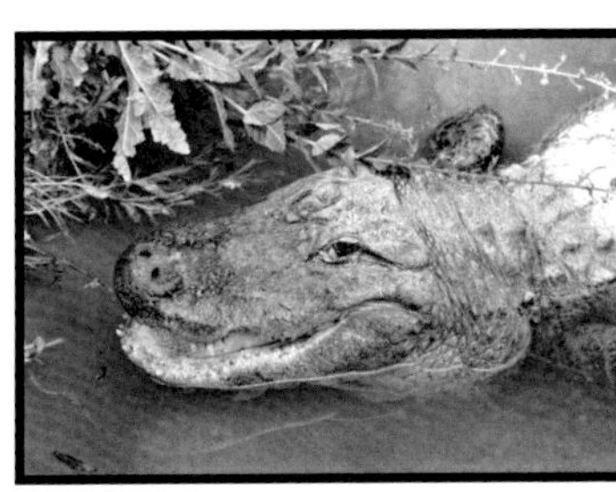
A Hungry Guy

Photo Op #1
The Reptile Ranch

The tour (and you must take it not because they threaten you or anything) has tons of photo ops and costs about $8. You can take all the photos you want and pretty much have all the time you want. A young boy led us on the outside tour and while he was very knowledgeable, the mothers in us came out while he was showing us **crocodiles** and **alligators**, getting way too close for comfort. There are also various kinds of **chickens, other fowl** (types we can't remember), an **emu or ostrich** (they look alike to us) and **Leo the Lion** along with several hungry looking **tigers** – all fenced in, thank you Jesus, with double fences in the case of Leo and the tigers. The young man assured us the chickens weren't fodder to feed Leo and the tigers. We were greatly relieved and just hoped the fences were good and strong. We've seen the footage of tigers attacking their trainers. Luckily, we left our whips, cargo pants and jungle hats at home.

Having finished the outside tour, we were led back inside the "Gift Shop" where they took us into the "Reptile Room," after a little lecture about not sticking our hands into cages. *Seriously?* I was already creeped out enough. Angie and Nancy were eager (*fools*).

Here in the Reptile Room it gets even weirder – **snakes, baby alligators**, some kind of **monkeys** and a **Komodo dragon**. While they were all in glass cages, (except when they took them out and asked if we wanted to pet them), I was busy checking out the floor for stray lizards or whatever. Could I say "eweeeew" one more time? Our funny little devil of a guide pointed to a hole in the wall and said a snake escapes occasionally. Nancy and Angie calmly said, "Oh, really?" That was enough for me and I high-tailed it outta there, while they all laughed at his little joke. Ha ha.

Photo Op #2
Meramec Caverns and the Zip Line

After exiting the Reptile Ranch with all of our limbs in tact, we decided to drive on to Meramec Caverns to see something advertised along the highway as **Zip Lines**. It was only a short drive from the Ranch (maybe 2 miles). For those of you not-in-the-know, Meramec Caverns is really a cave and famous Missouri landmark AND a hangout for people who like to wear flip flops, short-shorts, sleeveless undershirts and think gravy is a beverage and beer is breakfast food.

The Zip Lines run across the parking lot (very scenic and in case the line breaks they can scoop you up and put you right into your car) and then over the **Meramec River**. We watched lots of people climbing very tall towers, all for the privilege of jumping off and hanging on to a gear of some kind with a strap seat. Oh, I should mention that they did have on helmets so we guess that made it a safe venture. Interesting photo ops and the **people watching factor**... A+.

As we headed out to get back on Highway W, we spotted a gas station with a gigantic "Fireworks For Sale" sign. Yes, it was time for a Pit Stop. Did you know that you can actually buy $600 worth of pre-packaged fireworks and liquor in one spot? We desperately wanted some nourishment, like ice cream, but were afraid to look in the coolers in case they were storing the offering of "live bait."

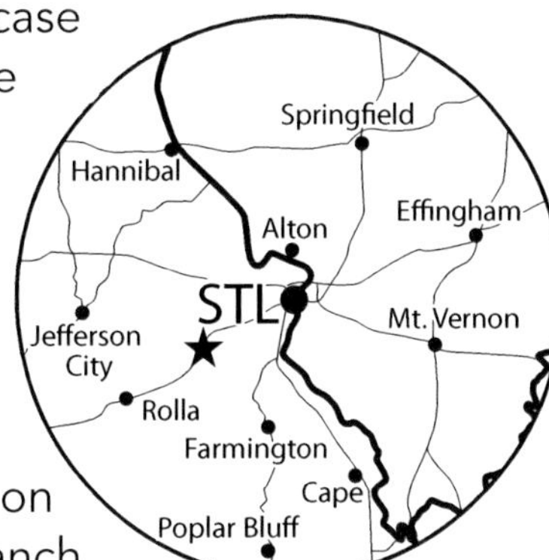

Approximate mileage from Downtown St. Louis: 62 miles

Directions: Take 44 west to Exit 230 and go left on Highway W and right on Meadow Drive. You can't miss the Ranch

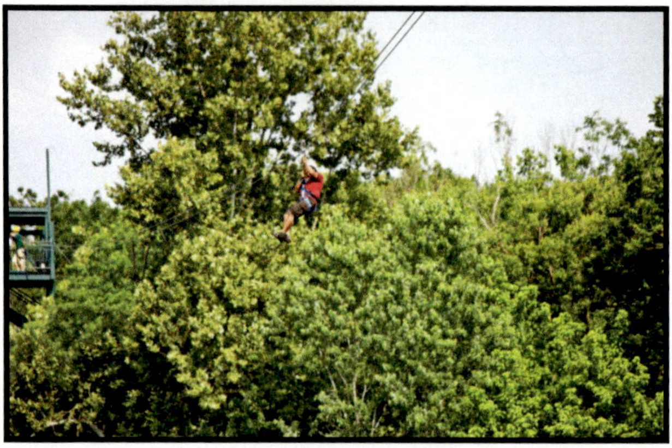

Zip Lining

because it is truly one of a kind and sits off to the left by itself. I wonder why? Here is an address and phone number: 275 Highway W, Stanton, Missouri. 573-927-6253

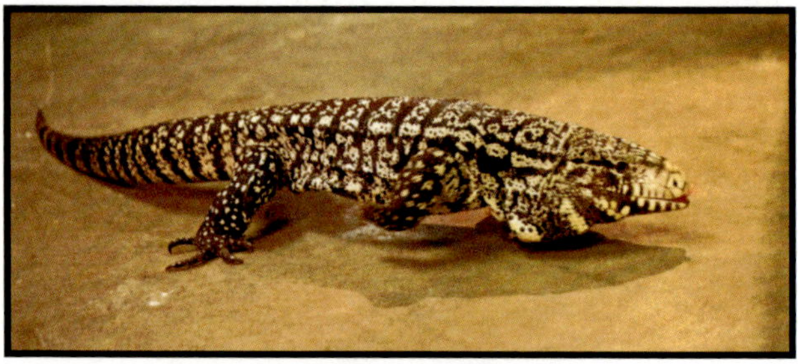

A Komodo Dragon (We Think)

If you really want to go to the Cavern and Zip Lines, exit at the Ranch and turn left. Meramec Caverns is about 2 miles farther.

Food: Really?

Handicap Accessible: Are you kidding?

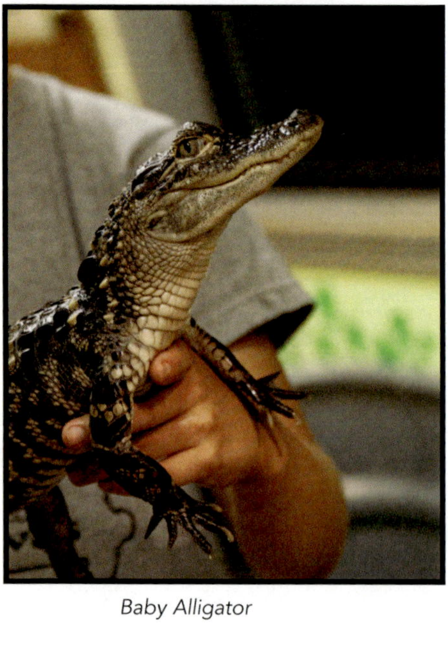

Baby Alligator

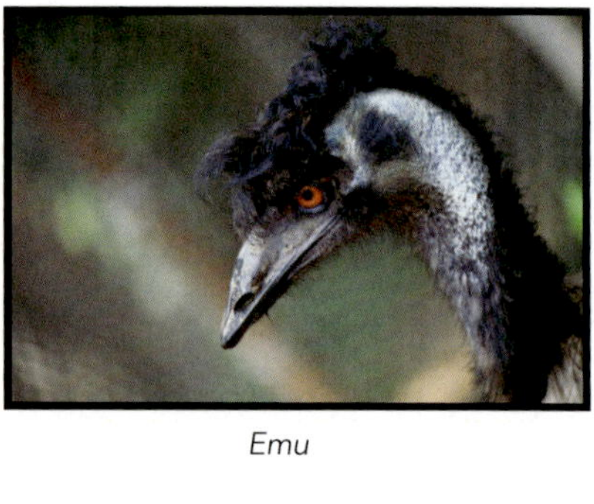

Emu

EIGHT

DeSoto, Missouri

DeSoto is another little gem of a town not too far out of St. Louis and it contains so many photo ops we had to mention this place.

Photo Op #1
The Little Deserted Mexican Town

There are several ways to get into DeSoto but to take in Photo Op #1, we want you to go in according to the directions below. We nicknamed this place "**The Little Deserted Mexican Town**" since the **red tiling**, **archways** and plaster-looking walls reminded us of Mexico. Of course, only one of us has actually been to Mexico and this may be as close as the rest of us can get. Okay, so there aren't any Mariachi bands serenading us and no Margaritas being served anywhere. Nevertheless, this is the only way we can describe this place. We did ask around in town about the history of these **structures** but the closest we came was that the land belonged to a church. Okay, so it's the ***Mysterious*** **Little Deserted Mexican Town**. There are a few grapevines off to

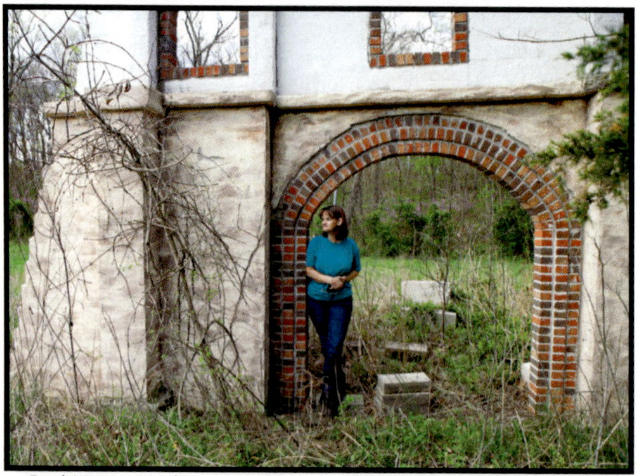
Bad Nancy Under an Archway at the Deserted Mexican Town

the side and it looks like perhaps it had once been home to motel, kind of like Coral Courts, but maybe not as much fun. There aren't any buildings standing, just tons of **archways**. This would be an interesting place to take family or senior portraits.

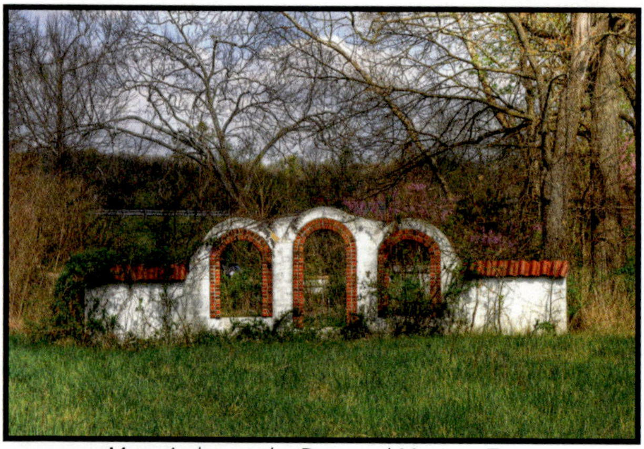
More Arches at the Deserted Mexican Town

There is also a **creek** running next to it with a tunnel under the road so this gives you another opportunity to shoot some interesting abstracts through the **tunnel**.

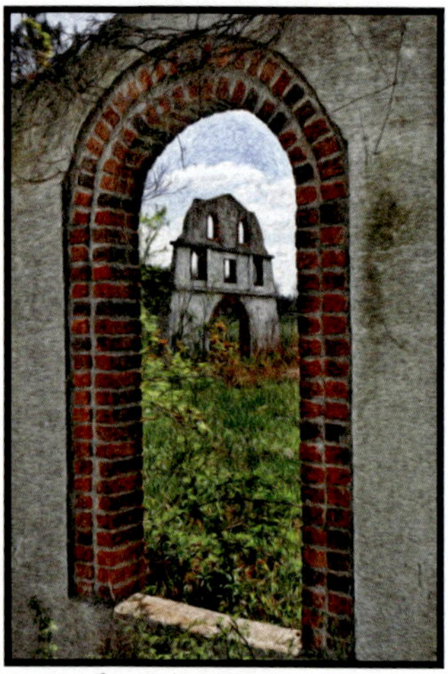
Scene from the Deserted Mexican Town

Caution – the best time to visit here is winter, early spring or late, late fall because most of the underbrush is gone.

Directions: Take 55 South to Highway 67. Turn right on 67 and in about 3 miles you will see an exit for Highway 110. Turn right on 110 and follow this road approximately 5 miles. Before you reach an entrance into town (there are two off this road) you will see, on your left, this collection of archways. Turn left (which is actually a back entrance into the Deserted Mexican Town) and make another immediate left which takes you on a little concrete road, right down into this "Town." Just park there.

Handicap Accessibility: Not good for people that have trouble walking or need a wheelchair.

Photo Op #2
Firehouse

While driving around town we went past the firehouse and since it was a warm day, all the bay doors were open and a fire truck was sitting outside. Nancy made a sharp U-turn on two wheels (probably a good thing it wasn't the Police Station) and said, *"I'm going in there and ask if we can shoot his racks.* (We are always interested in racks.) *I saw lots of bright yellow coats hanging up!"* When she makes up her mind, she makes up her mind.

This is the friendliest place in town and we spent quite a bit of time here. There was only one fireman on duty (they rely heavily on trained volunteers) and it was a slow day. He let us ask questions and take all the photographs we wanted! It made us want to hang around and wait for a fire (I know, this is a terrible thing to say) but we so wanted to photograph them in action. He told us that they actually have a photographer who volunteers his time to follow them to fires and take pictures. The fireman showed us some of this man's pictures

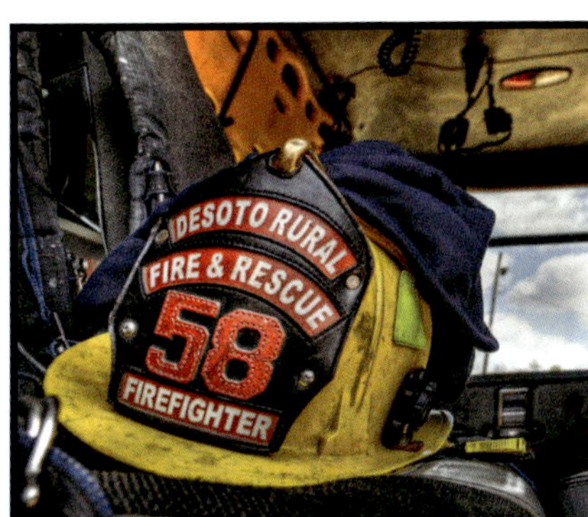

A Volunteer Fireman's Hat

and they were awesome!

Directions: Since there are two entrances we will tell you that one goes through the middle of town, next to railroad tracks. Very hard to miss. The Fire Station is down Main Street about halfway through town on your left. The other entrance we mentioned under **The Little Deserted Mexican Town** takes you on the left side of town. It's hard to get lost because the town isn't that big.

Handicap Accessibility: Definitely a good spot. There is a parking lot in back and once you have permission to shoot, there is a back door.

Photo Op #3
Joachim Park (off of West Miller Street and Joachim Creek)

While in DeSoto we saw a group of motorcyclists driving around so we decided to follow them. Hey, this was on the up and up! They always know the best places to go. Sure enough, we followed them to the edge of town and into a great park on the Joachim River. The river is perfectly clear with a rock bottom and a few people were fishing. We thought ahead for a change and brought a picnic with us. We parked, enjoyed the sunshine and scenery.

Handicap Accessibility: Perfect! There is a paved parking lot then paved pathways to the picnic spots and/or for strolling around.

Photo Op #4
Trains – WOO WOO

There are tons of train cars on the tracks, which run all the way through town, parallel to Main Street. Many years ago this was called the **Missouri Pacific Railroad** Shops and it's where box cars were built and repaired. Since you are not allowed "into the yard" we couldn't ask anyone if that is what's still done, but you can take photographs from the sidewalk. Gorgeous **colors** and even occasional **graffiti**.

Photo Op #5
Old Texaco Station

While you can't go inside, this is a **restored original – gas pumps** and all. There is a parking lot that surrounds the building and pumps so it's very handicap accessible.

Photo Op #6
Vintage Cars

On your way out of town, heading down Main Street, on your left is a Used **Car** Dealer and the many times we've been to DeSoto, there is always something **vintage** in the lot waiting to be restored. The area is not fenced in, but is posted so we just stood on the sidewalk and took some shots. No Big Bubbas or dogs chased after us.

Photo Op #7
Scenic Farm Country

This is a little drive well worth your time. My husband was a foster child and grew up on one of the **Centennial Farms** you will pass in this area. In case you don't know what Centennial Farm means, (I know you know that centennial means 100) it has been in the same family for over 100 years. Unfortunately,

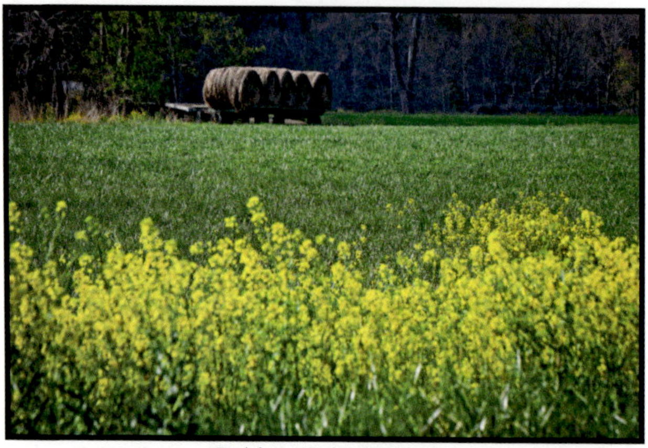

Field on Oakvale Road

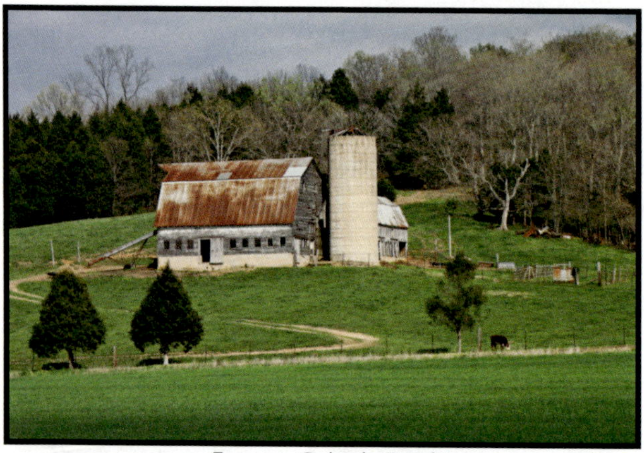

Farm on Oakvale Road

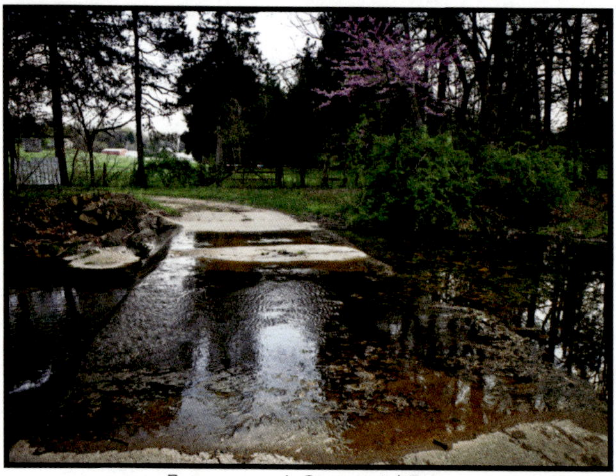

Entrance to A Centennial Farm

it is not open to the public and they don't like trespassers. We were allowed to go back to the farm only because my husband still knows the family. I can't divulge the family name (it's NOT Coday or Lister or Gellner in case some of you are detectives). There is a creek running in front and also one of those concrete slab bridges over the creek. If you find it, please don't drive onto the bridge – it's rather dangerous. However, you can stop and photograph the creek and any part of the farm you can see from the main road. There are quite a few **Red Bud Trees** in the spring – very **scenic**!

Approximate mileage from Downtown St. Louis: 45 miles

Directions to Scenic Farm Country: Go back out to Highway 67. Head south on Highway 67 from Highway 110 and in about 3 miles, turn left onto either Flucom Road or Oakvale Road. This is absolutely beautiful, **hilly farm country** with a couple of great **old barns** and even an old **church and cemetery** on these roads.

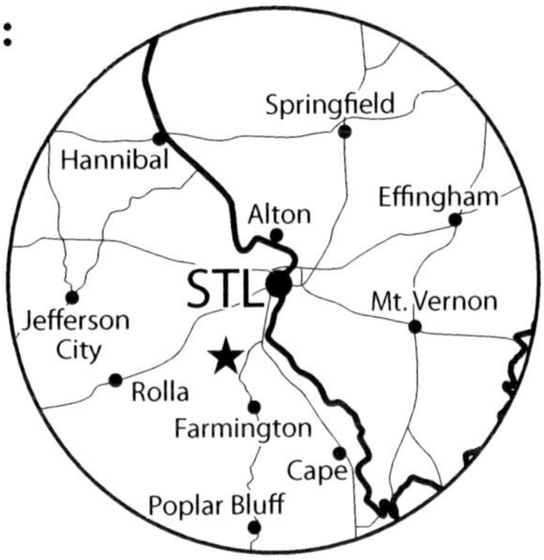

Directions to DeSoto: Take 55 South approximately 25 miles from downtown St. Louis until you reach Highway 67. Take this right, or south, for approximately 8 miles. Turn right onto Highway 110 and travel about 5 miles to Highway P. "The Little Mexican Village" will be on your left. If you want to go in to DeSoto you can follow Highway P. Or, you can get back on Highway 110 and take the next left turn, which takes you onto Main Street DeSoto. The town isn't that big. Following Main Street takes you by the rail yards, the old gas station, shops, Catholic **Church**, and the Arlington Hotel (built in the 1860's).

Handicap Accessibility: All photo ops are excellent, except for "the Little Mexican Town."

Food: Depends on the day you are in town. There is an old three-story hotel built in the 1860's in the middle of town called the Arlington Hotel Bed and Breakfast, across the tracks and visible from Main Street. We have eaten there and it's a fun place to grab a few shots. I don't know if they serve alcohol in the deli, but I think they do in the main dining room. So in grabbing "shots" you can perhaps do either kind.

NINE
Valles Mines, Missouri

Photo Ops and history abound in this little forgotten **mining area** and village. The multi-thousand acre tract is named after Francois Valle, who came from Canada to Kaskaskia, Illinois in the 1740's and is believed to have established a trading post at Valles Mines in 1749. Valles Mines is within the southeast mineral district in Jefferson, Madison, St. Francois and Washington counties commonly known as the Old Lead Belt. The Valles Mines tract was among the earliest clusters of mines operated during the French colonial period. **Rural decay** is everywhere.

Photo Op #1
The Furnace Tender's House

The Furnace Tender's House will be on your left as you enter Valles Mines School Road. While you can't go into the house, it's still an interesting stop. You can easily park on the side of the road.

Photo Op #2
The Valles Mines Smelter and Scotch Eye Furnace

This will be on your left, back in a field as you pass the Furnace Tender's House. Unfortunately, this smelter chimney has recently fallen down, in part. You can still see some of the stones and a sign on the fence says, "**Historic Structure** 1770 – Lead from This Furnace Used in Revolutionary War." It sits behind a small field that has a sign that says, "Charcoal Field 1830." We were told the miners later made their own charcoal to use in the Furnace.

Photo Op #3
The Lost History Museum

This structure is built around a **log cabin** that was built in the 1749 and while the **museum** is pretty primitive inside, it is full of **historical items** and the person in charge of this little bevy of buildings is delightful with his knowledge and family history of the area. He took us around to a few more buildings and **log cabins**, allowed us to take all the photographs we wanted and gladly answered all of our questions. Be sure to go upstairs. There may be a **ghost.**
Hint: While it's not required, he would greatly appreciate any kind of a donation to keep running this little privately-owned village.

Photo Op #4
The Pay Master's Station

This is the original building where the miners turned in their ore for pay. It was robbed many times and the **front door** has 1,000 nails driven into it to prevent robbers from shooting through the door. The sign out front says "Paymaster's Office – 1840." Since it is a nice **red color**, it makes a great shot and then there is that crazy door.

Photo Op #5
The Company Store

This is who the miners' "owed their soul to" (as in Tennessee Ernie Ford's song "Sixteen Tons"). They were given credit for supplies and food, which was then deducted from their pay. The original **Company Store** was destroyed by fire (I think) and this "new" one was built around 1840. **Great old structure**. The Museum has **original handwritten ledgers** from the **store** and **mine company**. While it's fascinating reading, we were intrigued with the beautiful handwriting! This is almost a lost art.

Photo Op #6
Slave Cabin

This little (very little) **log cabin** was used by slaves working in the mines. You are allowed to take all the photographs you want.

For All You ***Ghost Lovers*** ... There is a supposedly haunted railroad tunnel located about 2.5 miles south of Valles Mines. Since it was very muddy that day, we were told that it was kind of difficult to get back to this area so we decided to wait for a drier day. The **ghost** of a man named Bill is said to haunt this tunnel. At the **Lost History Museum** there are reports of a ghost that has been seen at the windows of this **historic home**, which dates back to 1749. It was the home of Francois Vallee, and during the Civil War a shoot-out between Union and

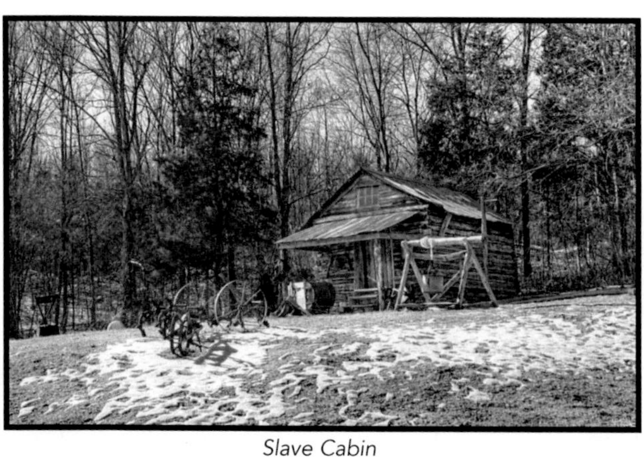

Slave Cabin

confederate troops took place here. The **ghost** is said to pull people's hair and paranormal photos have been taken. Boooooooh.

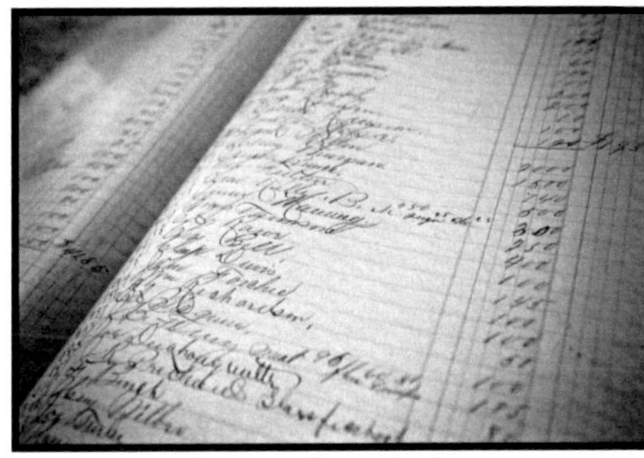
Country Store Ledger

You might want to contact the Museum before visiting any of the places we mentioned above to check for hours. Here are the number we were given: 636-586-3680 or 636-586-5573. There is also a **General Store** which lists this number but it didn't appear to be open. 573-631-6875

Approximate Mileage from Downtown St. Louis: 49 miles.

Directions: Take 55 South. Exit Highway 67 south and follow to the Valles Mines Exit. You will exit to the right, which is called V Road and make an immediate left onto Valles Mines School Road. Within a half mile you will see the first Photo Op – The Furnace Tender's House. The rest of the Ops are past this location.

Food: There are no restaurants in Valles Mines as of this writing. We went back on Highway 67 (North) and exited at Highway 110 – to the left. Follow 110 about 5 miles until you come to Highway 21. Make a left on Highway 21 (or south). In about 2 miles you will see a nice restaurant called "Get Hooked" in a log building. It is very clean and the food was good, again by our hungry standards!

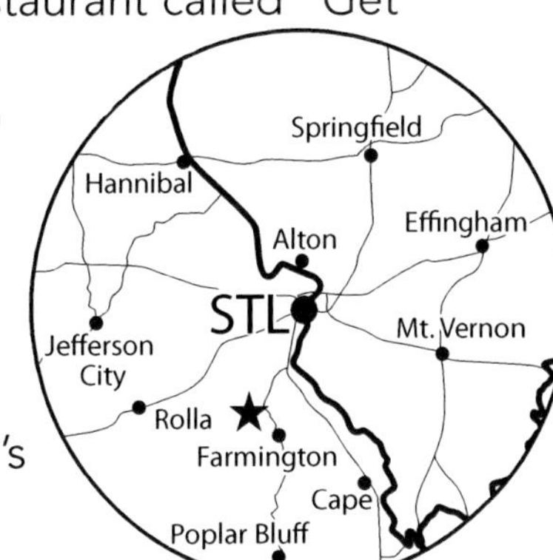

Handicap Availability: While you can see all the buildings from a car, it's obviously more interesting to go inside various structures; however, it's not a flat area so I don't think a wheelchair would move well.

Paymaster Station at Valles Mines

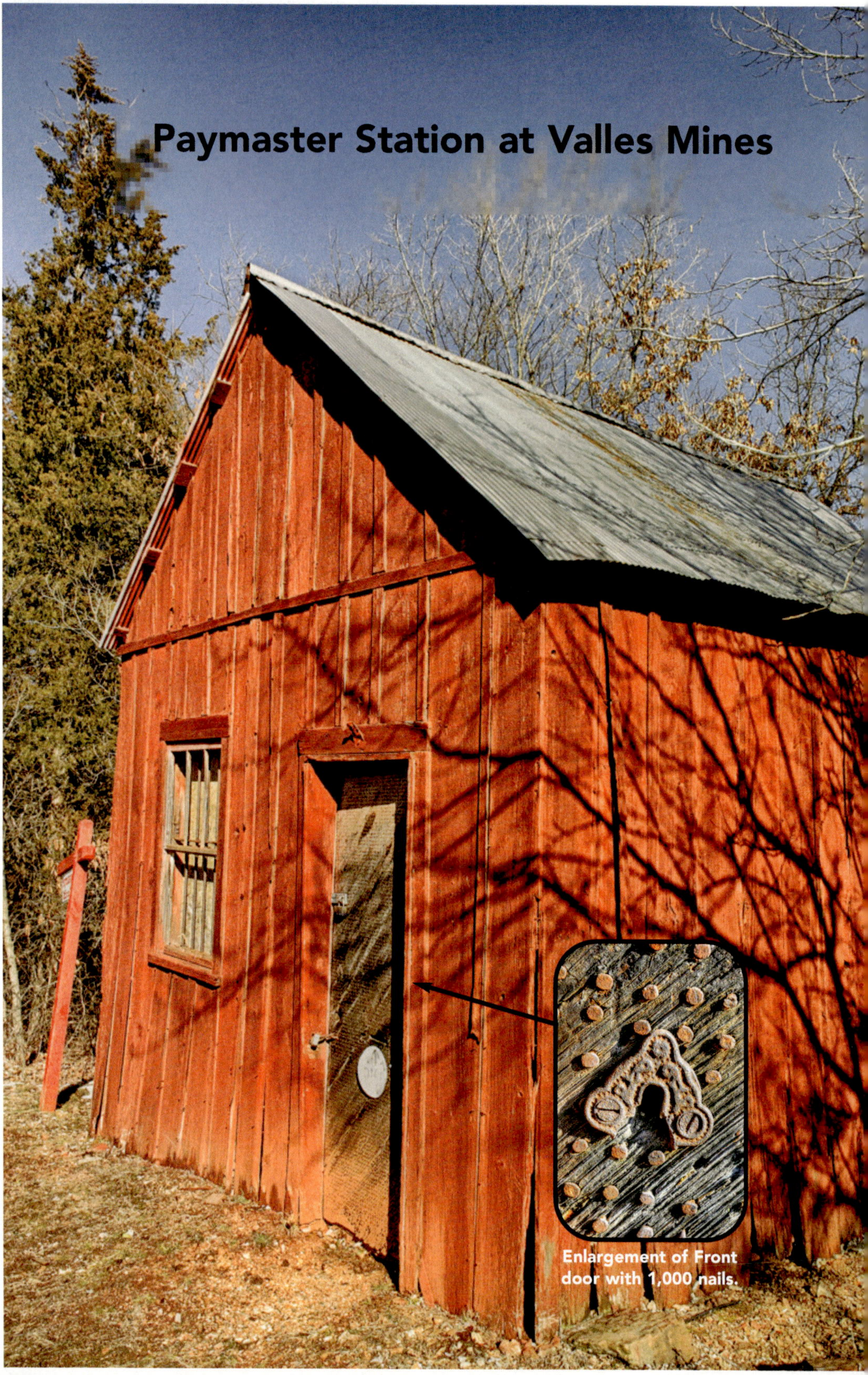

Enlargement of Front door with 1,000 nails.

TEN

Daniel Boone Home

Defiance, Missouri

We know you are saying, "What's so unusual about this place?" For one, it is rarely advertised and two, there are lots of great places to shoot and/or visit out in that same area. Plus, we do have a few tips and information to pass along.

We will start with the Daniel Boone Home, which is located down Highway F (plenty of signs mark the way), and we have included directions for those of you who may be from out of town.

There is a small admission fee to enter the home and surrounding village. Of course you have to go through the gift shop to buy the tickets, but it is well worth the price. We think our tickets were about $5/each.

Throughout the village you will see **old benches**, **farm equipment**, **flowers**, **brick fireplaces**, **split rail fences**, **textured sides of buildings**, **old windows/doors**, **barnyard animals**, and a **village green**, etc.

Lindenwood University, in St. Charles, Missouri, is doing a fantastic job of re-constructing a **village green**, along with buildings you would find in a town setting for the 1800's. You will also find: a **small white church, school house, log cabins, example of a detached kitchen, barnyard, houses, barn with mill stone, general store, and a covered bridge**.

The Bad News

You need to check the hours of operation before you head that way because they vary during the seasons of the year. Here's where you can check: www.danielboonehome.com

Even if DB's home and village are open, the outbuildings may be closed to the public. *Hiss Booh* to this we say, however, the barn is always open and there are plenty of photo ops. This didn't stop us from peeking in windows and trying a door knob or two. It's obviously more fun to go inside, which they allow, during special events and festivals.

The Good News

We have to tell you about a Christmas time event which only runs four weekend evenings in, what else, December. It is not well publicized and this event is guaranteed to melt even the scroogiest of Christmas hearts. Again, you can find a schedule at www.danielboonehome.com.

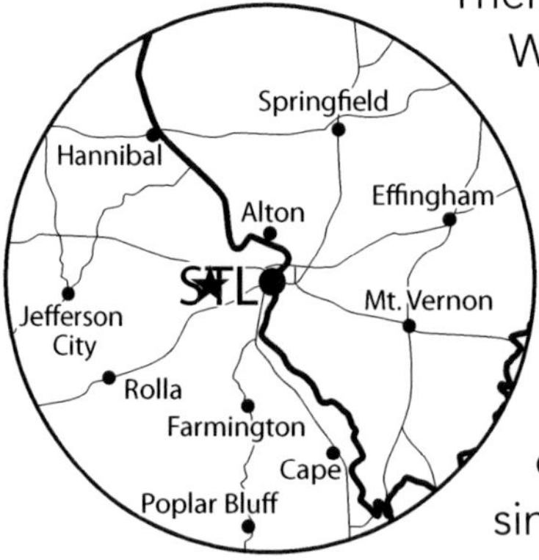

There is a charge of about $12/each and WELL WORTH IT! The house and village – in fact – everything – is lit by candlelight and lanterns which makes a Christmas Card scene. There is also a big bonfire on the **Village Green** and all the volunteers are dressed in period costumes. Folks are walking around singing Christmas carols and all the outbuildings are open with fires blazing in the **fireplaces** and decorated with natural greens, holly berries and plenty of **candlelight**. One year, a woman dressed in period costume, was baking molasses cookies from a 200 year old recipe in a **woodburning brick oven** next to the fireplace. OMG – talk about hog heaven. We each got one cookie but of course we could have eaten another dozen. She was also serving hot chocolate since it can be kind of nippy in December. Mark this one on your calendar!!

Approximate Mileage from Downtown St. Louis: 42 miles.

Directions: Take 40/64 West to Highway 94 South. Follow 94 until you get to Highway F (about 7 miles). Go right on Highway F and follow signs. Daniel Boone's Home is about 5 miles from F and 94 and will be on your left. The actual address is 1868 Hwy F, Defiance, MO 63341.

Food: You are in the heart of wine country and there are signs directing you to the various wineries.

Handicap Accessibility: Daniel's home is up a slight hill from the parking lot. All the pathways are lined with a fine chat mix and this is true for the little village in the back as well. The village is probably easier to access because the whole area is flat.

ELEVEN

Femme Osage, Missouri

This is a **quaint little town** off the beaten path that was settled by German immigrants in the 1830's. It sits down in a valley surrounded by the **rolling hills** of **Missouri Wine Country**. It is filled with a wonderful **stone schoolhouse**, a **white church** complete with steeple and **cemetery** which sits up on the hill behind the church, and an **old general store**.

According to history, the District of Femme Osage got its name from a young Native American woman of the Osage Indian Tribe. As legend has it, she was in love with a white youth who had been imprisoned by her tribe in a cave on the Femme Osage River. He was to be killed at a future festivity. (They certainly had strange ideas about "festivities.") As the story goes, in the night before the tribal celebration, she helped him flee and this didn't make the people of her tribe happy campers. One evening as she sat on the creek bank, longingly looking upon the Missouri River, in the hope that her beloved would soon return, she was struck on the forehead by a stone thrown by the shaman of her tribe. She fell into the river and

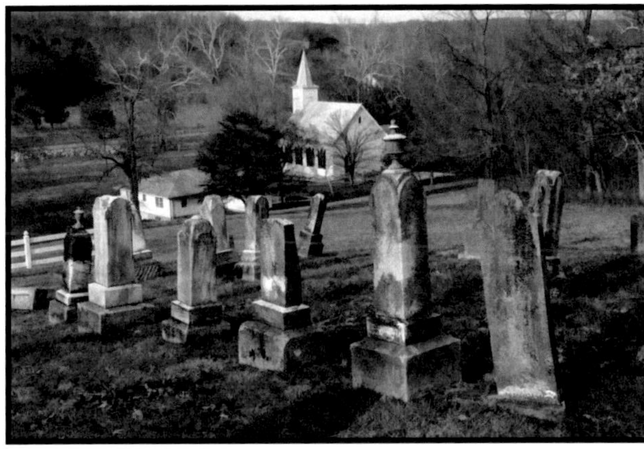
Church and Cemetery in Femme Osage

drowned in the creek near the mouth of the Missouri. She was later found by a farmer of French background. Upon witnessing the tragedy, he sorrowfully cried out, "It is a female Osage!" Okay, I didn't make this up.

A bonus: You are in the heart of **Missouri Wine Country** so we will list them for you in case you worked up a thirst taking photographs. There are 10 different **wineries**:

Chandler Hill Winery (off Highway F, 10 minutes from Femme Osage)
The Yellow Farmhouse Winery – Defiance
Sugar Creek – Defiance
Montelle Winery – Defiance
Mount Pleasant Winery – Augusta
Augusta Winery – (oh duh) Augusta
Augusta Brewery Company if you are looking for beer
Noboleis and Balducci Vineyards – outside Augusta
Blumenhof Winery – Dutzow
Cedar Lake Winery – Wright City

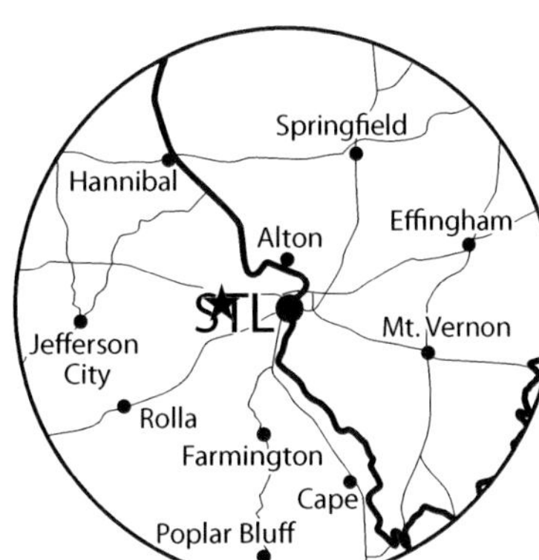

Approximate mileage from Downtown St. Louis: 48 miles

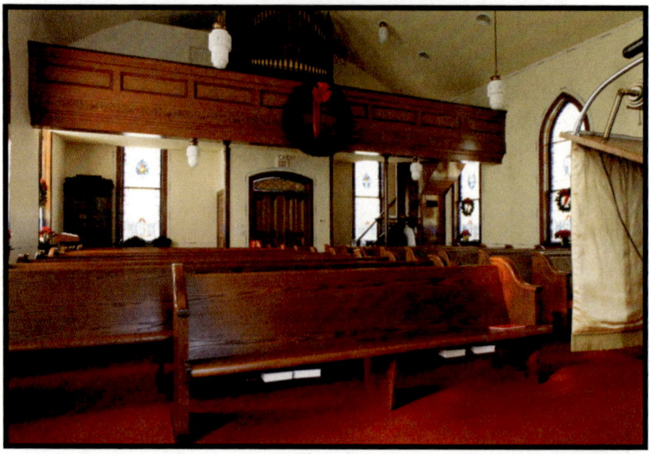

Church

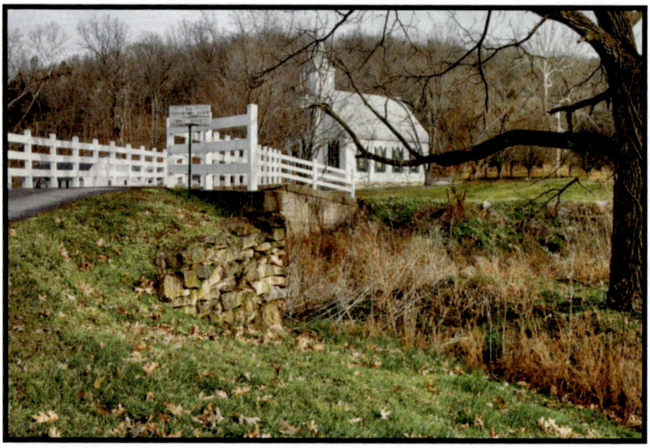

Church

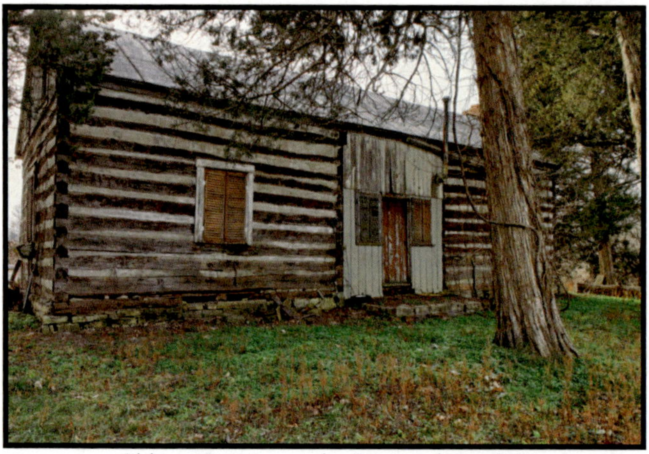

Old Log Structure at the Corner of T and 94

Directions to Femme Osage: Take 40/64 West across the Missouri River (through Chesterfield Valley) and exit at Highway 94 South (or left). Follow 94 all the way to Augusta. Stay on 94, past the Augusta exits, and take a right on Highway T then take a right on Cappeln Osage Road.

Handicap Accessibility: Femme Osage is very accessible as it is down in a valley and the town is flat. As far as the wineries go – you are on your own.

Food: There is nothing in Femme Osage but then you are in the middle of all those wineries ...

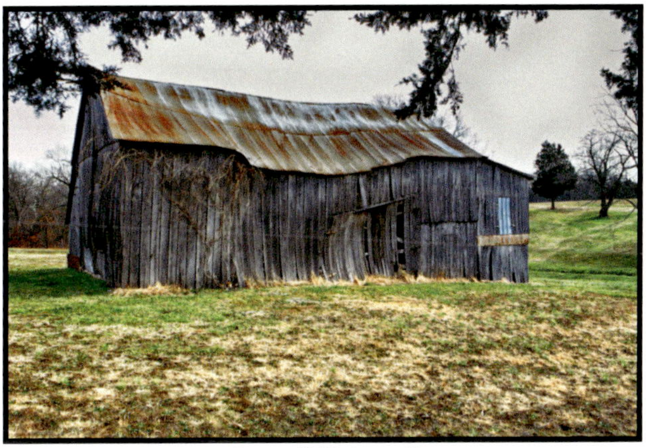

Barn off Highway T

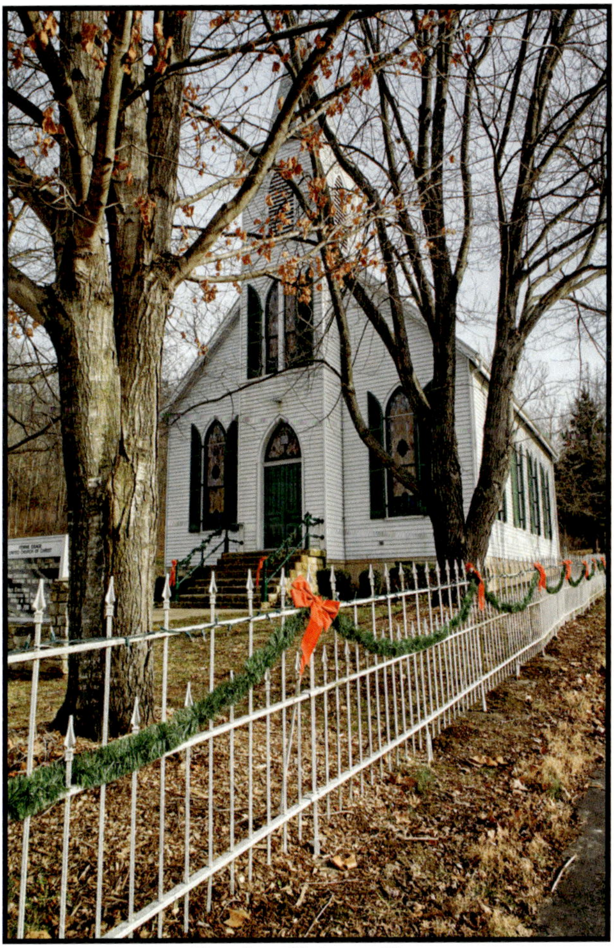

Church at Christmas Time

TWELVE

Defiance, Missouri

This is a strange name for a **quaint little town**. There are several great PHOTO OPS here so we had to mention this place.

Photo Op #1

As you arrive in town (from Highway 94 south) on your left will be a vacant lot with lots of great **old tractors** with beautiful (to us anyway) wheels, tractor seats, along with plenty of **rust** and **texture** as well as **color**. The lot is not posted and was mowed, so we parked and shot away.

Photo Op #2

Down toward the middle of town is an **old storefront** (last time we were there it was painted lime green) that you can't miss. It has a **front porch** and houses two businesses: **bicycle** renting and a **craft/gift shop**. This town borders the **Katy Trail**, thus the bicycle renting facility. You must walk behind this building where you will find several **scenic opportunities**, like a **foot bridge**, a **red shed** with an **old school desk**, a friendly **cat** or two and **flowers** (depending on the time of year you visit, of course).

Photo Op #3

You are now in the perfect place behind this old storefront to see a **scenic view**. From this position you can see flat fields with a single, lone tree and a **country gravel road** that heads down through the fields and actually ends up at the **Missouri River**. To get to this gravel road you have to get back on Highway 94, which is the main road through Defiance, then drive your car around the bend and past the Biker Bar, which is not the official name. Anyway, this bar has a parking lot that is usually filled with – what else – **motorcycles**. Hey, we're not stupid. The country gravel road entrance is through this parking lot. Drive on through the lot and head straight on the gravel road. Then, just pull off to the side somewhere and start shooting. We've been there when the field is full of corn; and also when the field is plowed under. If you are lucky and there are lots of clouds in the sky and the **river bluffs** (Missouri River) in the background plus that lone tree – well, you are in business as this makes a great **scenic shot**.

Photo Op #4

The next place is a **deserted old home** a little way past Defiance (on 94 south of Defiance about 2 miles) and on your right. This place is only good for shooting during the late, late fall through early spring. It gets terribly overgrown in the spring and summer and we don't want to have to fight the underbrush. I am purposely not using the word "snake" because that would only encourage Angie to go tromping through in hopes of finding one.

Nevertheless, this is a fabulous **old rundown deserted 2-story house** that we are guessing is circa 1900ish. There is a "For Sale" sign in the yard so we pretended we might be interested in buying, in case anyone stopped to ask what we were doing there. It's never happened, so far. We absolutely do not

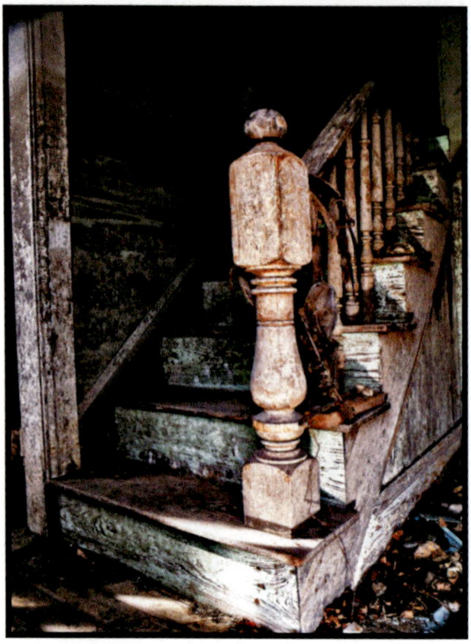

Staircase in the Abandoned House

recommend going into this house since "rundown" means exactly that. However, the front door is off its hinges and open so you can see a marvy (I'm boring myself with the word "great") **old staircase**, plus peek into several rooms from the front door. You will see wonderful **texture, architecture, peeling paint, color,** etc. Around the back of the house is a great (there I go again) shot of an **old window with the panes broken** out and the remnant of a curtain, which blows with the wind. Very spooky!

From this position (behind the house) you will also see the remains of an **old barn**. By the way, this makes a wonderful HDR shot, for those of you into that. If you are not, or don't know what in the hell I'm talking about, don't worry. **Texture and architecture** galore!!

There were one or two other **outbuildings** but they were falling down. While walking around places like that watch where you are stepping. People used wells back then and didn't always secure them. Wells are usually deep so do you get our message?

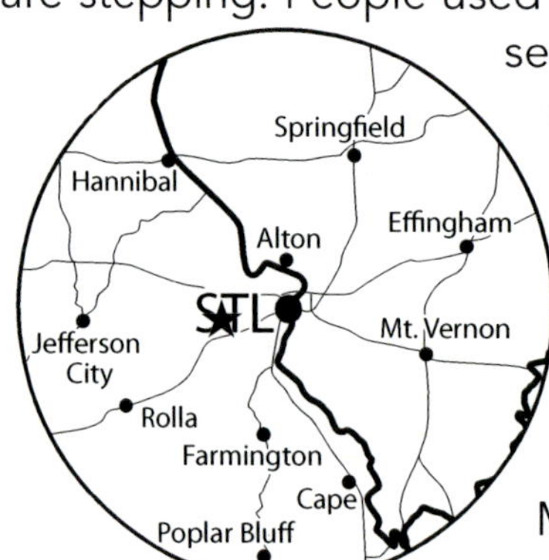

Approximate mileage from Downtown St. Louis: 38 miles

Directions: From St Louis take 40/64 west. You will cross the Missouri River (there's a bridge so it's not difficult to actually cross the River) and about the second exit (there's so much building/expansion going on in this direction that it's hard to keep up). Anyway, you want to exit at Highway 94, and go South. Once on 94 it's about 10-15 miles until you get into Defiance.

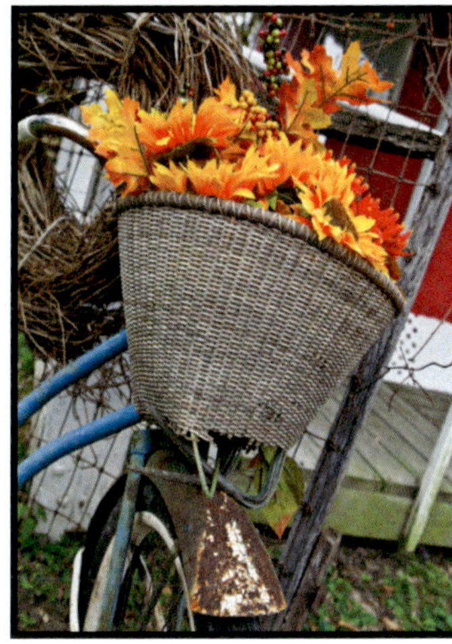

Bike Shop in Defiance

Food: You are in wine country and will actually pass a winery or two before you get into Defiance. We recommend the Biker Bar, which I mentioned earlier in this chapter. As I said, this is a destination for people who like to ride **motorcycles**. If you are into taking pictures of bikes, this is the place. Plus, the food is good old-fashioned bar food – you know – hamburgers, french fries, and beer. Everyone is friendly and not once did we feel like we would be kidnapped and forced to join a

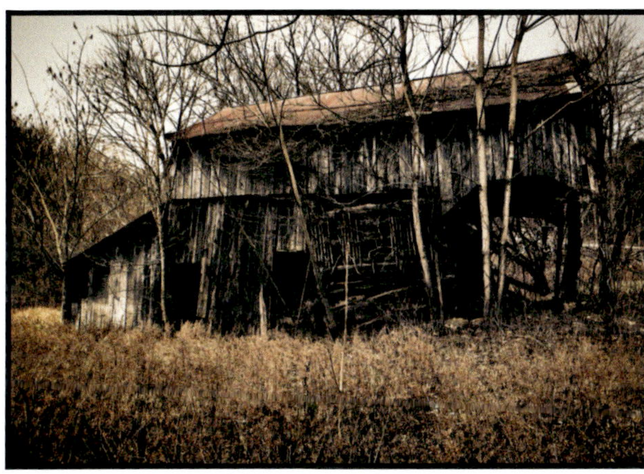

Old Barn on Highway 94

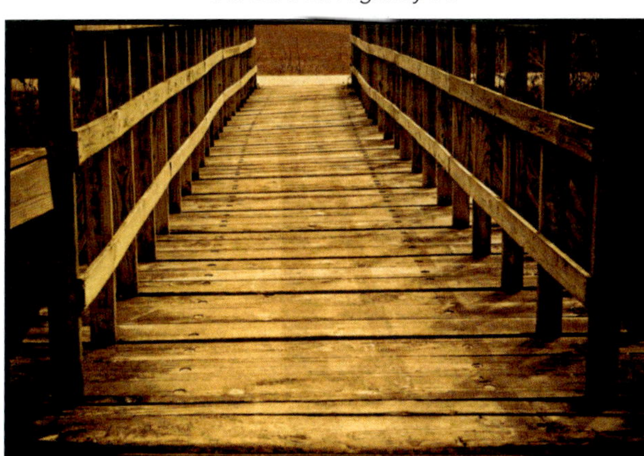

Behind the Bike Shop in Defiance

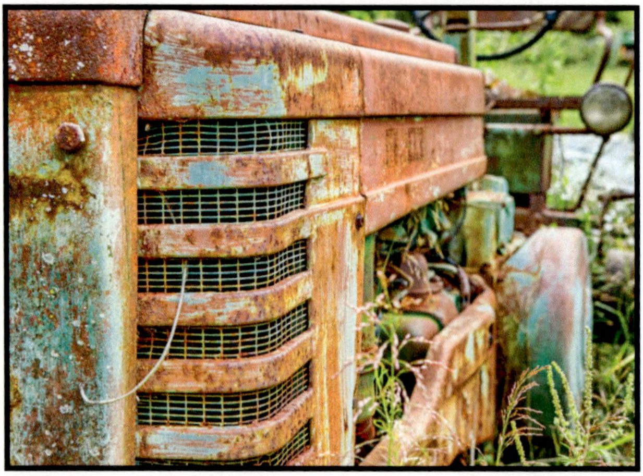

Rusty Tractor in Defiance

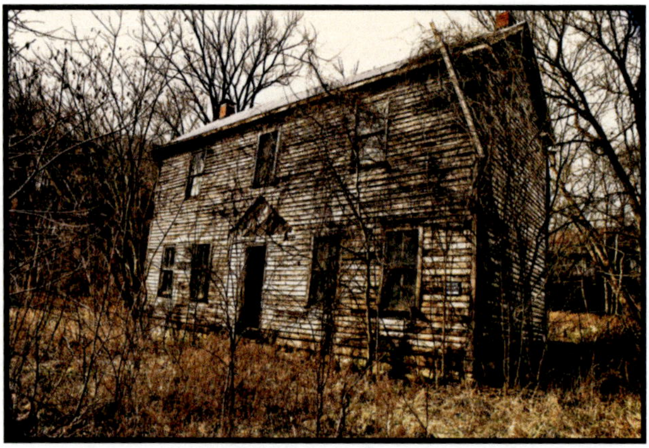

Deserted House on Highway 94

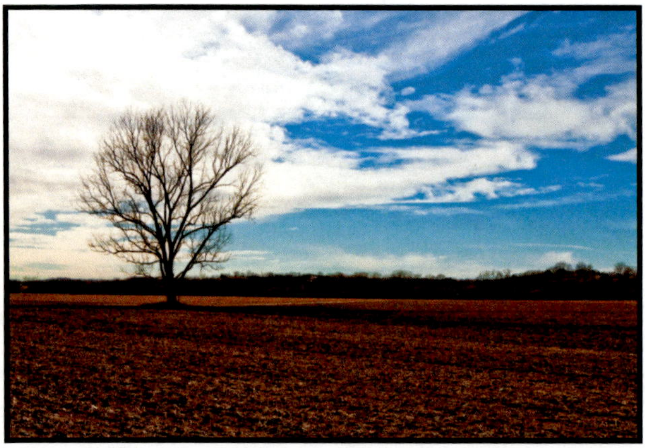

Field Behind Defiance

biker gang.

Handicap Accessibility: We would say that the only place not wheelchair accessible is the old two-story house. The rest have roads right next to them, but no sidewalks. There is a lot of traffic through Defiance (especially on the weekends due to all the wineries), but most traffic slows way down because one, there is a speed limit; and two, it's illegal to run over someone.

THIRTEEN

Caledonia, Missouri

You will be heading down Highway 21 South and it is possible that you might have driven through Caledonia on your way to Elephant Rock State Park or Johnson Shut-Ins. Highway 21 runs right through the middle of the town, which is a place that has remained virtually unchanged since the 1800s.

There are 33 homes and buildings that are on the national historic register.

Your first stop should be at a **general store** called "**Old Village Mercantile**" which is in the middle of town, on your left. It is owned by Steve and Nina Gillum and when you walk through the door, you will truly feel like a kid turned lose in a candy store! Nina keeps the store stocked with every possible kind of **candy** imaginable and you can just grab a bag and go to town. There are also home-baked goods, including my personal favorite – fudge!

For those of you not into treats (no one we know) there are many **antiques** for sale all over the store, as well as numerous

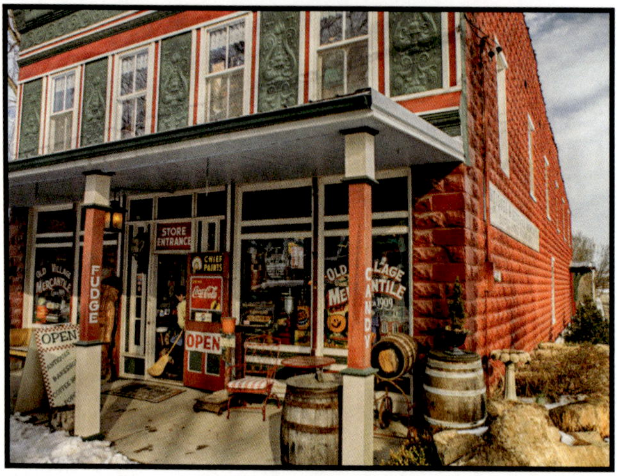

Old Village Mercantile

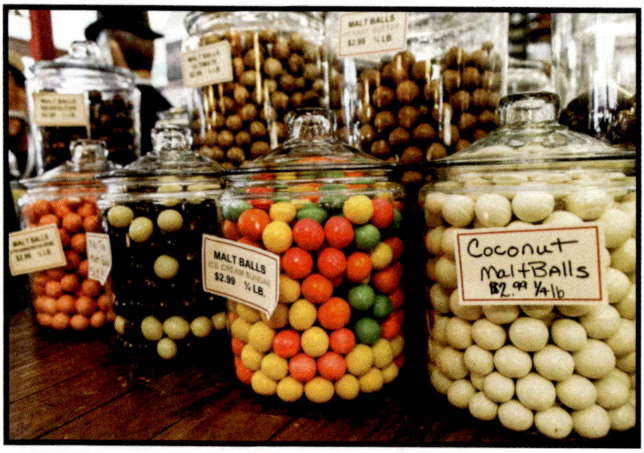

Candy!

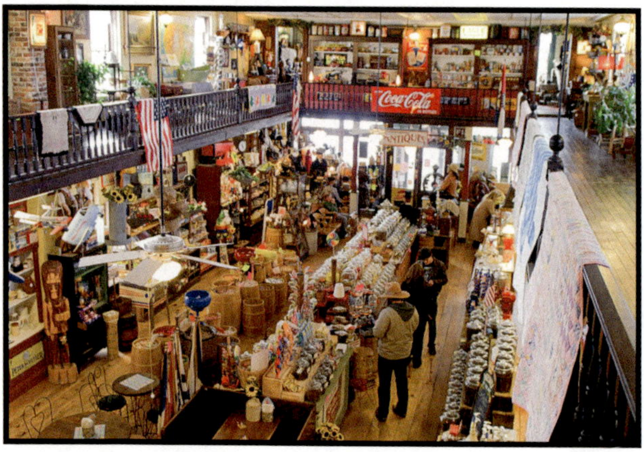

Inside the Old Village Mercantile

photo ops, including a great old **staircase**, **coca-cola memorabilia**, **jars of colored candy** as well as many antiques. Steve is the "antiquer" and keeps the store well stocked. This is also a great place for more information about the history of the store, as well as other places to visit in town, including a **log cabin** jail.

When Thomas Flanders traveled to Caledonia in preparation for its listing in the National Register of Historic Places, he wrote "The houses, streetscapes and landscapes they constructed remain, in great measure unchanged, from the nineteenth century."

The village of Caledonia (population in 2000 was 158) is located in the Bellevue Valley in Washington County. The village was founded in 1819 by young Alexander Craighead, who opened a frontier store on Goose Creek and platted the town of Caledonia around it. Craighead, possessed of impeccable high Scotch-Irish family credentials, named the town after the Roman Empire's Latin name for Scotland. The builders of Caledonia's houses "*cleaved to that chaste style of the early nineteenth century that Thomas Jefferson defined as proper for the Republic. The families must have been not only conservative in taste, but singularly devoted to a classical tradition in keeping with their Latin name, Caledonia (a rare place name for the United States).*" *When strolling through Caledonia, you will see the influence of Greek Revival Style* **architecture**. *Almost every house has a Greek Revival Style front door entryway."* In 1992, Mr. Flanders continued "*Caledonia is different. It looks different. Most obvious to the visitor perhaps is that it remains 'unspoiled'. Not only is it free of modern franchise glitz and roadside*

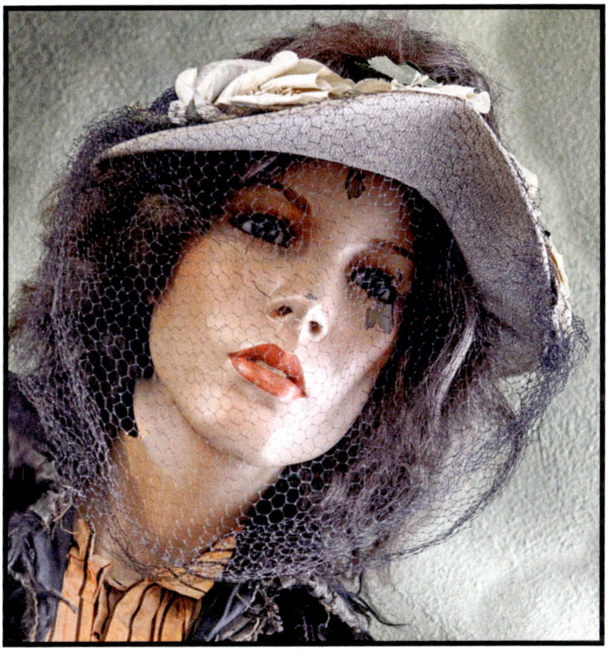

"Lady" in the Old Village Mercantile Store

'conveniences,' but it retains in its streets, lots, dwellings and public buildings, its ***barns****,* ***gardens****,* ***fences****,* ***walls****,* ***yards*** *and walks, the imprint of its history. Still evident in its landscape is the intention of its founders that it be spacious, rational, enlightened, and Protestant Christian."* Many of these old homes have been lovingly restored and now serve as antique shops or restaurants. There is an **old**, **green farm wagon** sitting in town, which makes a good photo op in the fall, when the trees are in brilliant, full color.

While in Caledonia, visit the Bellevue Presbyterian **Cemetery** and the **church**, the oldest protestant cemetery and church in continuous use west of the Mississippi River.

Caledonia has several festivals during the year. For more information visit: www.caledoniamo.org or 573-779-3907 for the Old Village Mercantile.

Approximate mileage from Downtown St. Louis: 85 miles

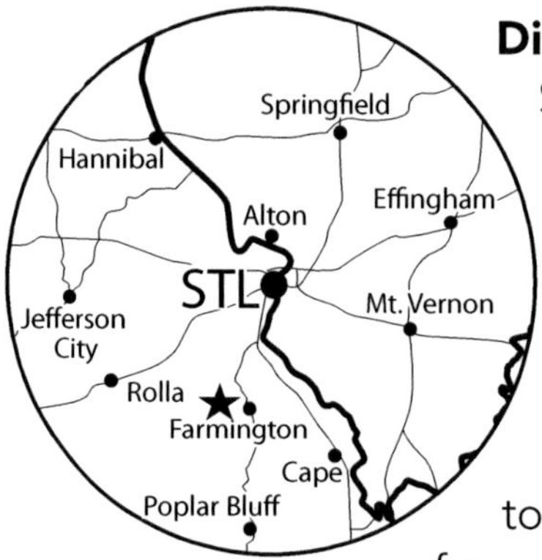

Directions: From St. Louis, take 55 South for approximately 30 miles. Take exit 174B for Highway 67 South toward Farmington/Bonne Terre. Take exit MO-32 and turn right.

Or, Take Highway 21 South, straight to Caledonia, which is about 60 miles from Highway 141 and 21.

Handicap Accessibility: Excellent as the town has sidewalks and is on fairly flat ground.

<u>**Food**</u>**:** There are several places in town and we would be hard-pressed to choose.

FOURTEEN

Potosi, Missouri

Every time I hear the name of this **quaint little town** I think of cereal. Now I'm really showing my age, but remember Post Toasties? They don't make cereal here but it is a very **old town** with again, lots of photo ops. Potosi is named after a town in Bolivia. Besides **antique shops** with very reasonable prices, we might add, there are quite a few restaurants and original **old buildings**.

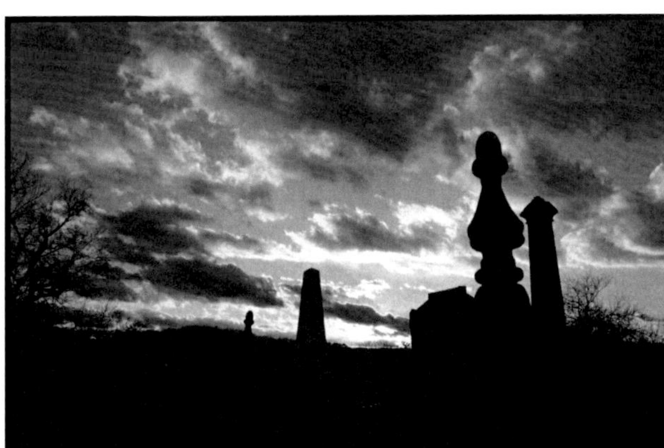

Cemetery in Potosi

Drive through the center of town (see directions below) and on your right you will see a **cemetery** and above it a great **old brick Presbyterian Church**, built in 1832. To get to the entrance, pass by the cemetery, the next

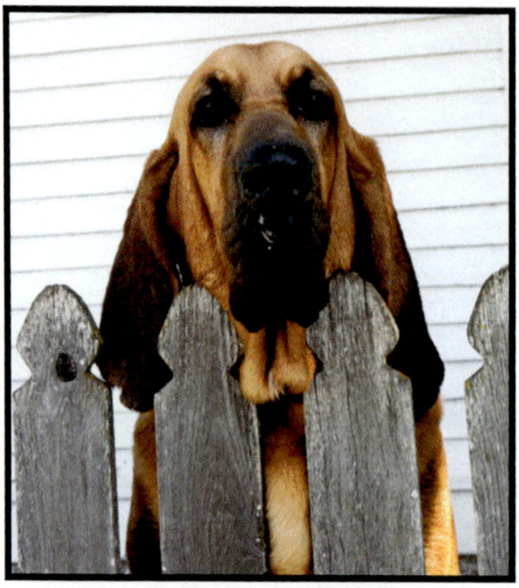
Blood Hound

road to your right will take you around to the front. I am assuming you are weird like us and enjoy reading old **tombstones**, but maybe not. We've been there several times and the last time was late afternoon. This was the BEST because the sun was highlighting all the tombstones – weird, huh? But, nevertheless, see our photos and judge for yourself. Plenty of old **iron fences**, too.

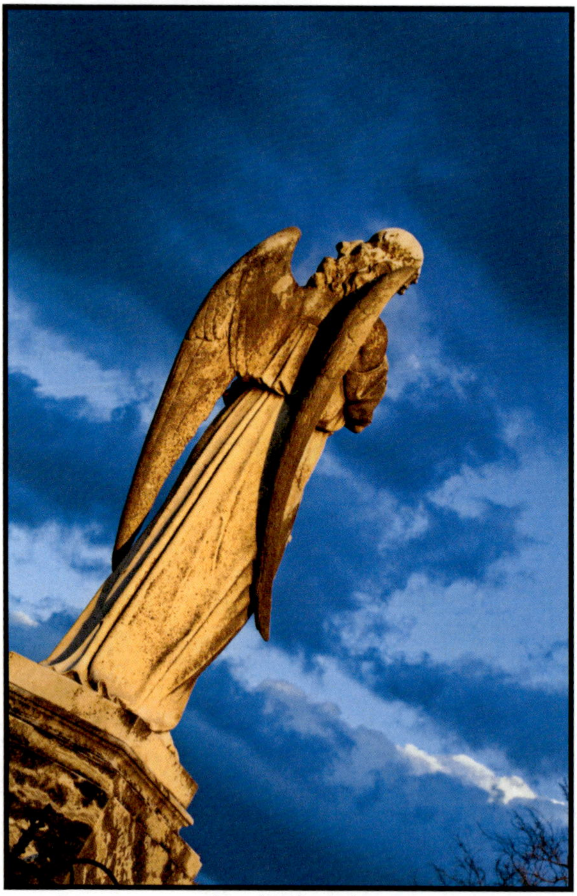
Angel in Sunlight

If you are an animal lover, there is a great old red colored **Blood Hound** that lives across from the church and he loves to pose for pictures, while putting his front paws up on his **white picket fence**. The old church has great **painted and weathered front doors**, but is not open to the public. Darn.

Celebrity Alert: In 2011 an 1800 lb. boar (no, not your mother-in-law) was killed near the Potosi Airport. Authorities didn't say what flight the boar was on. Seriously, for an amazing picture, go to google and search "wild boar, Potosi, Mo." Urban legend? You be the judge.

Approximate miles from Downtown St. Louis: 75 miles

Directions: The easiest way is to take Highway 21 South. From the intersection of **Highway 141 and 21 it is about 30 miles** to Potosi. You will come to a stoplight at the intersection of 21 and Highway 8. There will be a sign indicating "Potosi." Make a right and follow this street which takes you right into the main part of town.

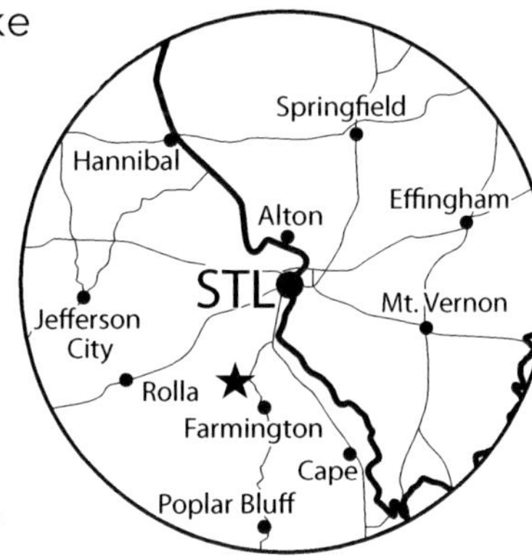

Handicap Accessibility: The cemetery is not great due to all the hills; however, there are sidewalks in town and the rest can be seen by car.

Food: Oh yeah, plenty. We ate at a good Mexican restaurant, Dos Primos on East High Street, which was very clean and the food was good. There are several other restaurants in town, too.

FIFTEEN

Downtown St. Louis

You're going to be sorry if you skip over this part because you think you've been everywhere in the City. We think, thanks to a lot of friends who are city rats, you will find a surprise or two. If not, well ... we can't win them all.

Photo Op #1
Graffiti Wall

Colors, colors, colors all courtesy of local **spray paint artists** along the flood wall down by, (where else would a flood wall be), the **Mississippi River**. You can't miss the Graffiti Wall (which is actually the flood wall as I've said before). The paintings change all the time so if you see something you like, you'd better photograph it quick, because the next time it will be different. This is also a great place to take **portraits**. Warning: Do not go there after dark!

You will notice that there are gaps in the flood wall and it's safe to take your car between these openings and then you can actually see the river and all the cool **industrial sites**, plus big strands of **old chain** used to hook **barges** and **tugs** along the river, **rope**, an occasional **propeller**, and general **junk**. The only time we've ever been stopped is by a security guard wanting to know if we were going to fish. We wouldn't eat fish out of the Mississippi, let alone know HOW to fish. When we told him we were just out taking pictures, he said, "Have fun." So we did.

If you are into history and **rusty**, old things, a unique thing happened the summer of 2012 while we were in drought conditions. Many years ago the **U.S.S. Inaugural (World War II mine sweeper)** broke lose from the main area of the Riverfront, hit a bridge and sank. It is now visible and lying on its side. The best view of this is by a Fred Weber Construction site. There is a yellow dock behind this building and a perfect view of the Inaugural.

We will tell you that the area is obviously posted "No Trespassing" but during the weekend no one seems to be around, or at least they are not pulling huge trucks in and out of there.

Directions to the Graffiti Wall: Everyone knows about the famous Riverfront down in front of the **Arch**, so just follow this road to the right or south of the Arch. The wall will obviously be to your left and it runs for a good mile or so.

Food: Too many places to mention. If you are new to town, the area to the North of the Arch is called "The Landing" and it's filled with lots of old buildings, the **Metrolink Station, architectural** items and restaurants.

Handicap Accessibility: Very good because you can actually stay in the car and shoot from the window.

Photo Op #2
Semi-unknown Deserted Graffiti Buildings

These buildings are uber (notice I hip I am) cool, but not places you want to go alone. We usually have several people with us since these locations are fabulous for **urban** portraits and shots of **eras gone by**. There are old **loading docks**, tons of **graffiti, great lighting, stairs, windows, chipped paint**, and **texture** galore.

There is another **graffiti building** right across from the one mentioned above. Same great stuff!

Directions: The street right in front of the Arch runs north and south – east would obviously put you in the Mississippi River. We gave you directions to the Graffiti Wall up above, only this time you will go north (instead of south) and follow it about 1.5 miles from the Arch. You will notice that you are now in an area that's obviously deserted. You will take this street until you can't go any farther. These graffiti buildings are on your left. There is a small road that you can park on and the City has now smoothed out a huge dirt mound so the buildings are viewable from the street. Oh, and you will have a great view of the new suspension bridge being built over the Mississippi River.

Food: Naw, you wouldn't want to eat down there.

Handicap Accessibility: Walkable with only a slight incline. We don't think you could get a wheelchair into these buildings.

Photo Op #3
Old Stone Church Shell

Talk about **arches** and old **stone buildings**, this one takes the cake. It is located close to the Fabulous Fox Theater and is located at the corner of North Spring and Washington, which is right off of Grand Avenue. The church faces Spring and it's easy to park on the street, right in front of the church. Hard to miss. Oh and did I mention there is no roof on this structure? It's kind of fenced in, but not really, so its easily accessible. Another great place for **portraits** and **arch-way** shots.

Directions from Downtown St. Louis: Take Washington Avenue west and stay on until you reach The Fox Theater. Grand Avenue runs right in front of the Fox. Stay on Washington, cross Grand and the Church is at the corner of North Spring and Washington.

Food: There are several restaurants along Grand and we like the Koda Grill which is right across from The Fox. You might want to check the hours. There are a few other restaurants on Washington Avenue as well as Olive, which is one block south of Washington.

Handicap Accessibility: You could take shots from the car but if you can manage a few steps, you can get right into the building.

Photo Op #4
Crown Candy Kitchen

A wonderful, **historical** place with the best chocolate malts in town, to say nothing of their bacon, lettuce and tomato sandwich with almost a full pound of bacon. Can you say "Oink?" It's also a great place for **nostalgic** shots of **table juke boxes** and great **antique booths** for seating. The lighting is pretty decent so you wouldn't necessarily have to use a flash inside.

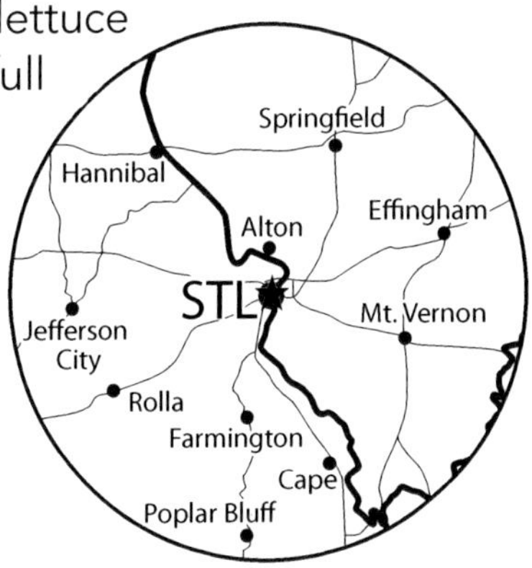

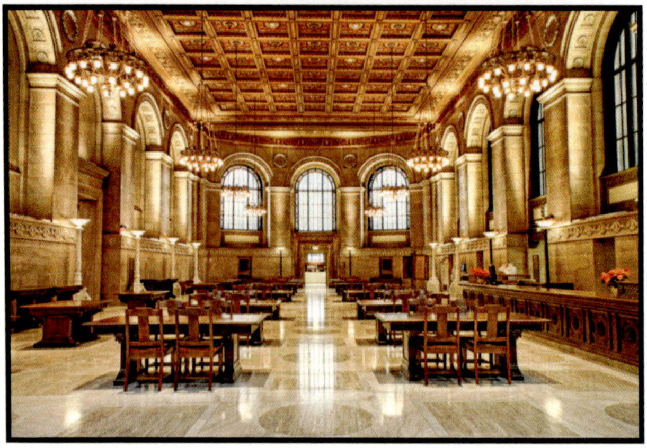
St. Louis Public Library

This is located in North St. Louis and the address is 1401 St. Louis Ave. You can park close, right on the street.

Photo Op #5
The Zoo

I know, I know. We said we didn't use "typical" tourist places that we complained about earlier in the book; however, here's the BIG SECRET! You can enter the Zoo at 7:00am using the back entrance, which really isn't like a typical back entrance. The front of the Zoo that faces Highway 40/64 is considered the official, main entrance, so this entrance is on the opposite side (the one that faces the Art Museum).

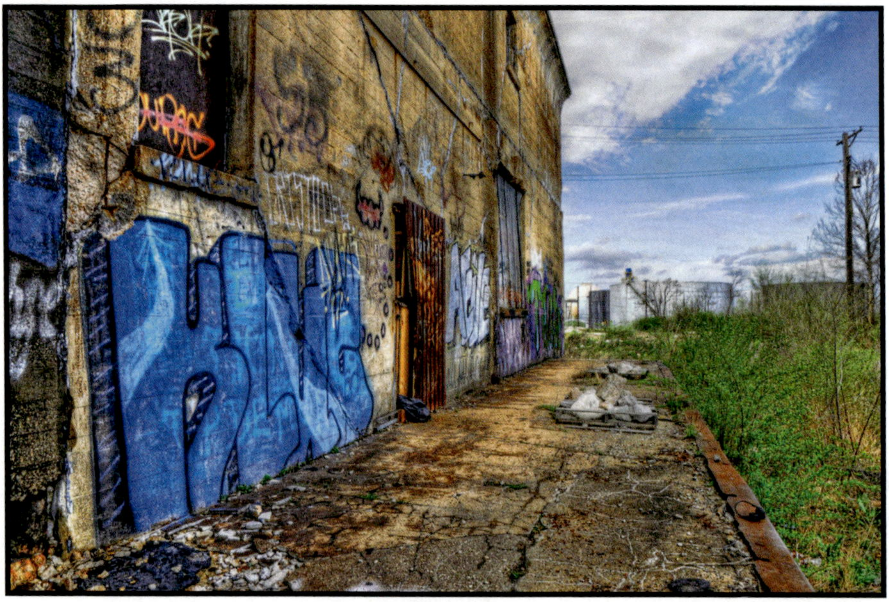
Graffiti Building

Now we know that 7:00am is early, BUT, there are no people around and it's the time of day when all the big **cats (lions and tigers)** are out and active. Plus, and this is a big plus, the parking is FREE in the lot attached to this back entrance. Normally if you get there around 8:00am you have to pay $15 to park, but not at 7:00am It's FREE – hurray!! Do check ahead for winter hours.

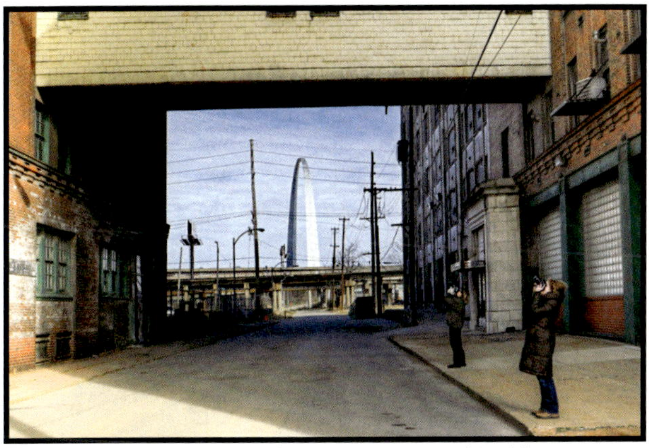

Judy and Angie Shooting a Deserted Building

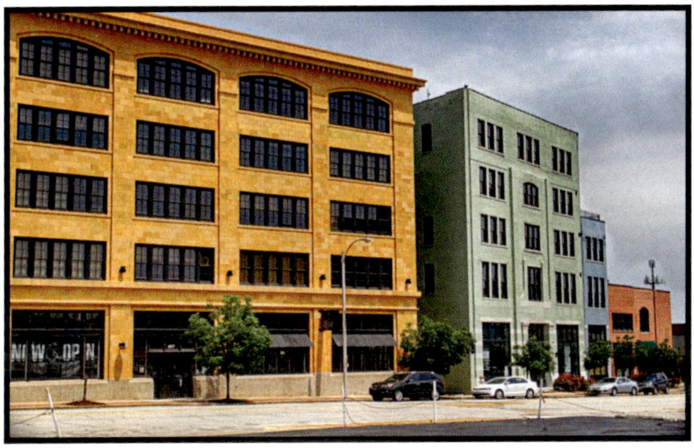

Colorful Downtown Buildings

Directions: If you are new to the City and coming from the downtown area, take 40/64 West and exit at Hampton (north). If you accidentally pass that exit, you will see the Zoo on your right. Just take the next exit and wind your way back into the park. There are plenty of signs.

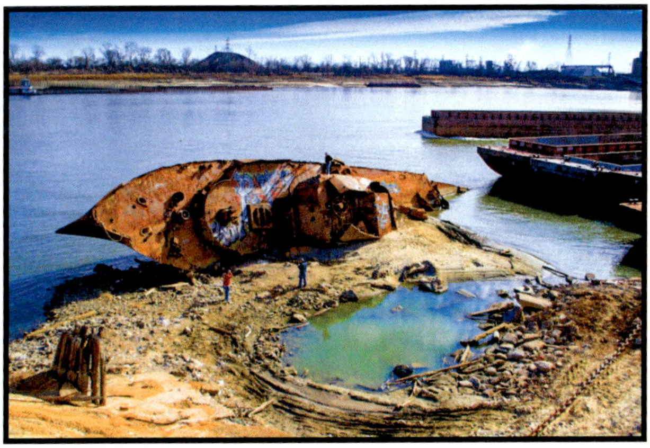

U.S.S. Inaugural. Notice People Standing by the Ship

SIXTEEN
Crown Ridge Tiger Sanctuary
St. Genevieve, Missouri

Photo Op #1
Crown Ridge Tiger Sanctuary

We think **tigers** are absolutely magnificent and this is the perfect place to see them. They are in huge outdoor sanctuaries and apparently treated very well. The Sanctuary's mission is to provide a permanent home for **exotic cats** that have endured neglect, abuse or undesirable homes. They strive to provide these cats with a healthy lifestyle by providing the best vet care, diets and activities.

While they are caged behind two heavy wire fences, we were able to get some great shots while they lounged. We had to pay for the tour and it was well worth it. While it is difficult to get good shots through wire, somehow we managed by putting our lens up close to the wire. We used our telephoto lens all the way to maximum focal length and used manual focus.

There are several other photo ops on the road out to this Sanctuary and we also recommend you visit the town of St.

Genevieve if you haven't done so. St. Genevieve was settled by the French in the **1700's** and if you love **architecture** of that period, this is the place.

There are lots of old **barns** and on Highway B we found a great shot of an **old rusted truck.**

Photo Op #2
Shoe Tree and Shoe Phone Line

This is located on the way to the Sanctuary (along with **great, scenic wine country**) on Highway B, off 32. As we were driving down B, we noticed about 10 pairs of **shoes** that had been thrown over **phone lines**. A startling sight so we decided to pull off onto a little gravel driveway. There we noticed a single tree, loaded down with all kinds of shoes (A real **shoe tree**). Nancy saw a pair she considered going after! Just a fun place to take a few shots.

Photo Op #3
Riverfront in St. Genevieve

St. Genevieve is, of course, right on the **Mississippi River** and they run a **ferry** over to Illinois. Head down to this area (plenty of signs) and you will find a place where they store **railroad cars** and our personal favorite, **cabooses**. We took some fun **sand sculpture shots** on the bank of the Mississippi River and then headed over to explore the railroad cars.

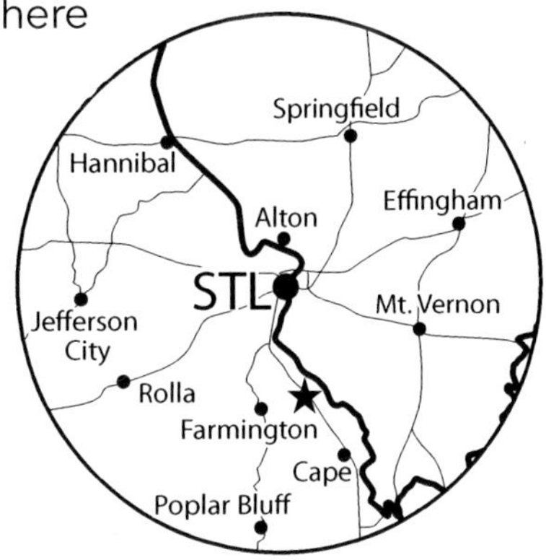

Approximate mileage from Downtown St. Louis: 64 miles

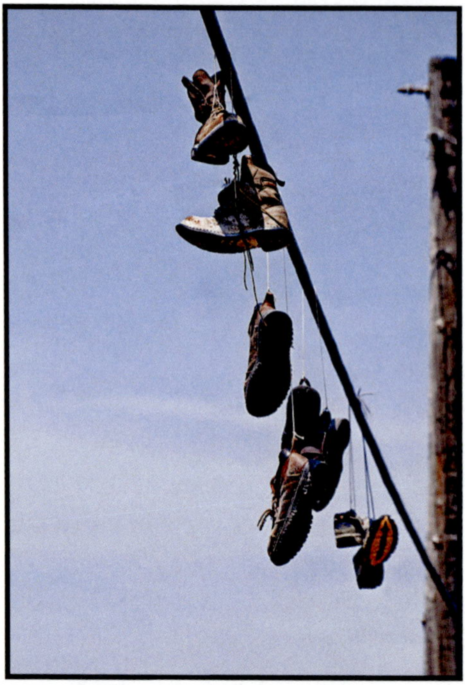

Shoes on a Telephone Wire

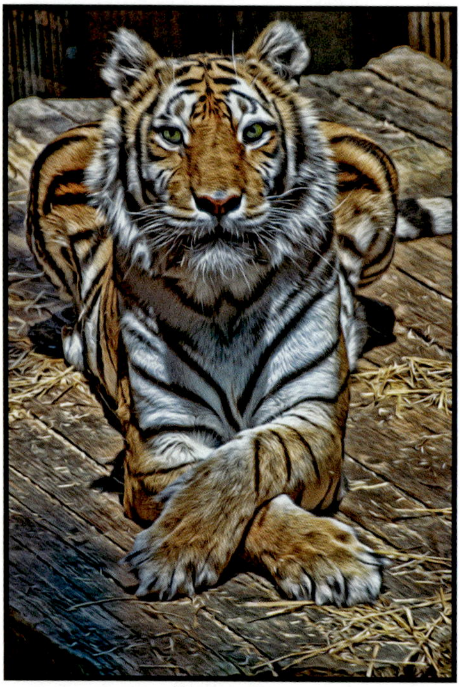

Tiger at Rest

Directions: Take 55 south to St. Genevieve and exit right on Highway 32. Then immediately turn right on Highway B. Follow B about 8 miles – the shoe tree and shoe phone line is on this stretch. This road may also be called WW. (It is Missouri) Nevertheless, there are signs for Chaumette Winery (which is where the Tiger Sanctuary is located) – go that way. Here is the address: 19620 Route B, St. Genevieve, MO 63670 and a phone number as they do have set hours – 573-330-7334.

Handicap Accessible: It's very hilly, but paved down to the actual tiger area.

Food: While we didn't eat there, the main building has a restaurant and it looked very inviting. This is wine country so you can pretty much have your pick of good places.

SEVENTEEN

Clarksville, Missouri

Highway 79 runs north up the **Missouri River** (which runs into the Mississippi River) and you can go as far as Hannibal, but for purposes of this book and not overwhelming ourselves, we are going to focus on some great places to stop on your way north, and then Clarksville itself. The Highway 79 corridor includes artists from coast-to coast who have moved into the area including Clarksville, Louisiana and Hannibal.

Photo Op #1
St. Paul Church

As you are heading north, St. Paul road will be to your left. It's kind of hard to see as there is only one little sign. The drive back to St. Paul's **Church** is very **scenic** with **rolling hills** and **farm land**. The Church was founded in the 1800's and although we didn't go in, we did spend some time wandering around the **cemetery** and reading old **tombstones**.

Photo Op #2
Annada, Missouri

Population 200. We actually met the former mayor of Annada when we stopped to marvel at a great **junkyard** filled with an **old school bus, rusty tractors** and **trucks, old farm equipment** and just good, general, photographable **junk** complete with **peeling, faded paint and texture**! We usually try to gain permission to be on someone's property and the former mayor was more than generous. He also had a great, **old, old house** and while we didn't go in (didn't look terribly safe) we had a great time photographing **old windows, doors**, etc.

Photo Op #3
Clarence Canyon Wildlife Preserve

Across Highway 79 from Annada is this easy-to-get-to Wildlife Preserve with drivable roads. We stopped to photograph all kinds of **ducks**, along with a **woodchuck**, and other **waterfowl**. There is also a small building with information available.

Photo Op #4
Barns

We had to mention that there are quite a few beautiful **old barns** on Highway 79 with places to pull off and take photographs.

Photo Op #5
Clarkesville

Several years ago we found a restaurant in Clarkesville called "Overlook Farm" owned by Nathalie Pettus. Nathalie is a powerhouse of design and creativity.

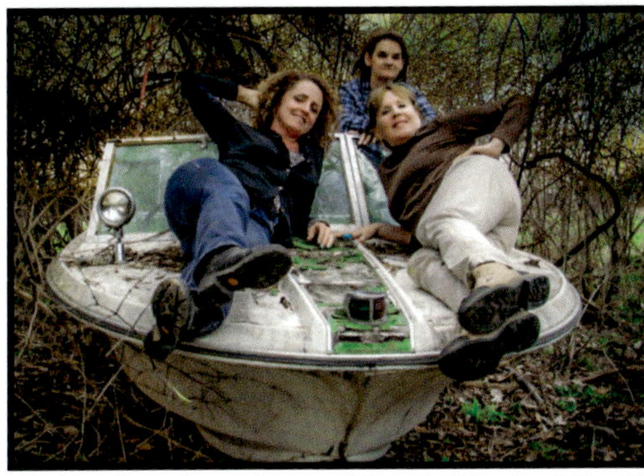

Bathing Beauties on Deserted Boat in Woods off Hwy 79

We had driven to Clarkesville for something we saw advertised as the **Sunflower Festival** and we unknowingly parked next to a restaurant owned by Nathalie. As we were getting out of the car this vivacious, attractive woman intercepted us in the parking lot asking if she could help us with anything. This was our lucky day! Not only did Nathalie give us directions, she got into her car, asked us to follow and proceeded to take us on a fabulous tour of her many properties (we think she is practically renovating the whole town). These properties include **bed and breakfasts**, **gardens, historical homes, benches, a tree swing, a gigantic chess set, scenic overlooks and farms** ... it was a wonderful tour. She then turned us loose and said to feel free to photograph whatever we wanted and to take all the time we wanted. Now, this was music to our ears. Oh, and we did find the **sunflowers**.

As we never missed lunch, we ate at Nathalie's **Overlook Farm Restaurant** and found the food to be quite good, to say nothing of the extremely beautiful **outdoor settings** that Nathalie is always in the process of creating. There is a great **craft/gift store** connected to the restaurant.

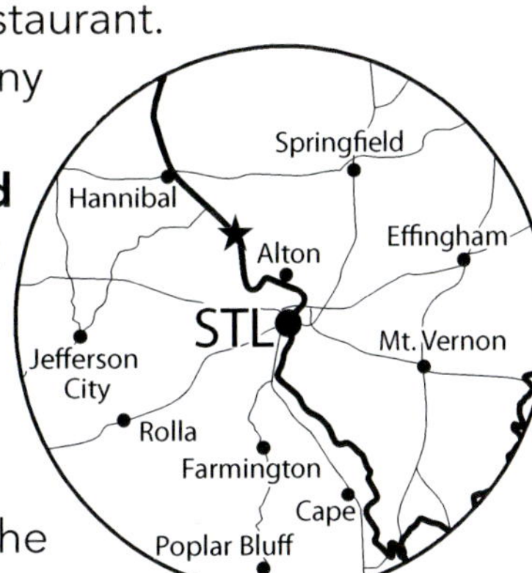

Over the years, we've been back many times and are always surprised at all the new construction in this great **old town**. Oh, and you can rent **bikes** at Nathalie's if you wish.

The **downtown** and **riverfront area** is an artist haven with many fine shops. And, you must drive up into the

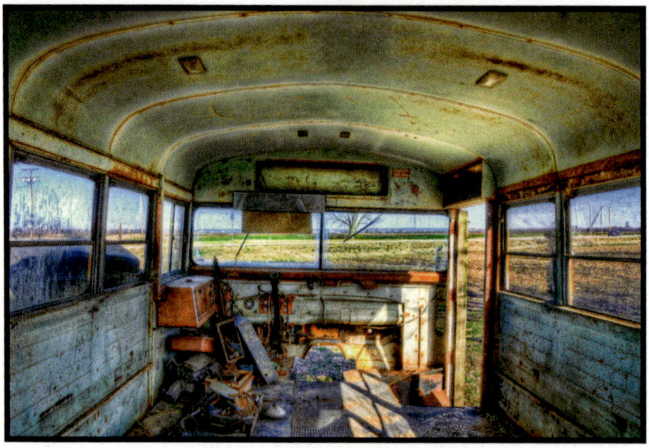
Inside School Bus in Annada

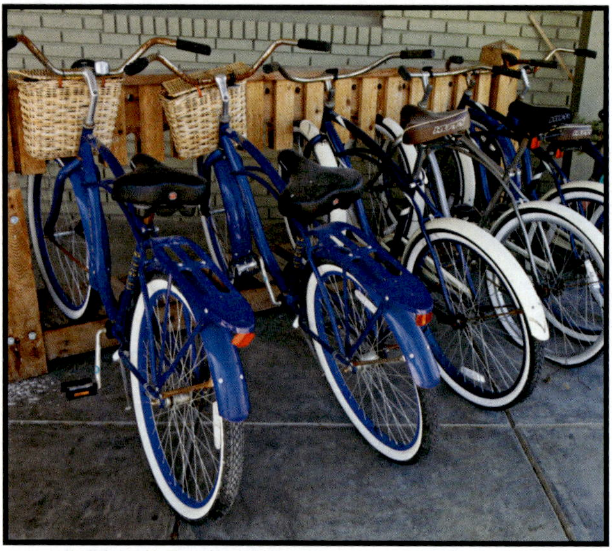
Bikes at Overlook Farm Restaurant in Clarksville

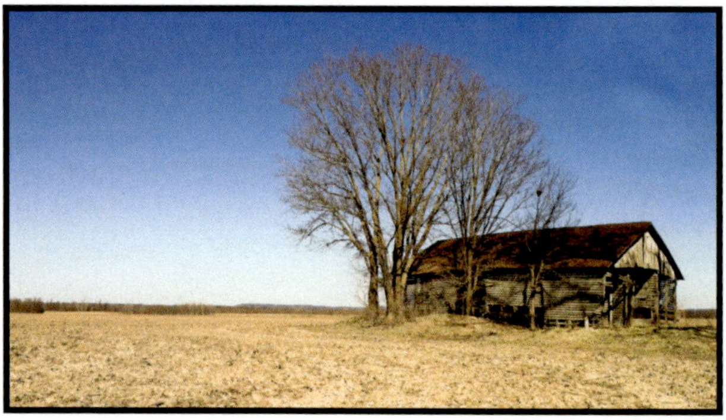
Off Highway 79, close to Annada

neighborhoods to envy their views of the Mississippi River. There are gorgeous **old homes, brick, paint texture** and reminders of life during an earlier era.

Some of you may have heard of the famous Clarkesville (newly renovated) **Sky Lift,** which gives a great arial view of **Lock & Dam #24.** Now this thing was popular back when I was in high school so good grief, that makes it and me antiques. Fortunately, the chair lift has been recently renovated (wish I could say the same for me) but I am not a fan of heights so maybe someday I will re-live my high school days.

Eagle watching is very popular here during January and February.

Approximate Mileage from Downtown St. Louis:
75 miles

Directions: From St. Louis take 70 West across the Missouri River into St. Charles. You will travel about 5 miles from the Bridge. Exit on Highway 79 North. Stay on 79 for about 45 miles.

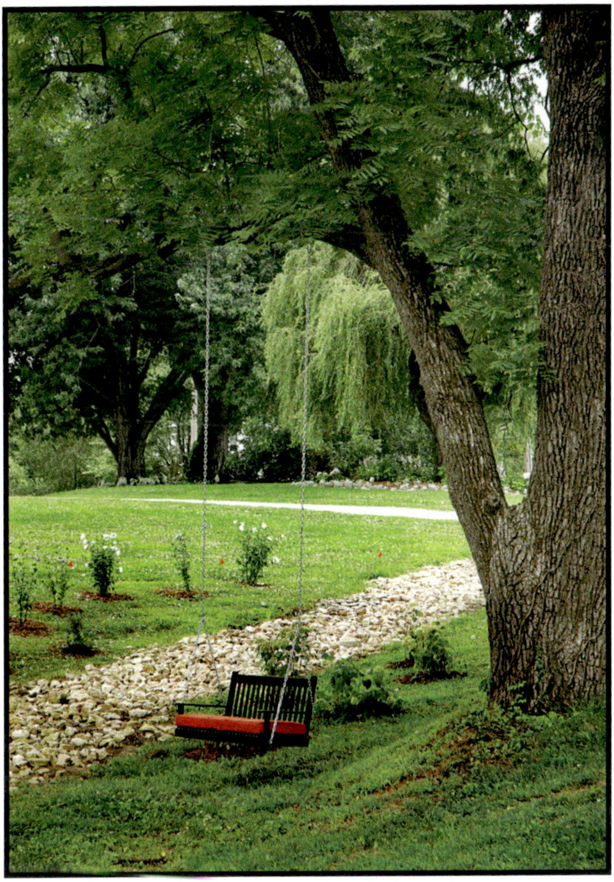

The Swing at One of Nathalie's B&B's

Handicap Accessibility: Most of the above is on flat ground so we would say this rates a "very good."

Food: You bet – Overlook Farm and say hi to Nathalie Pettus!

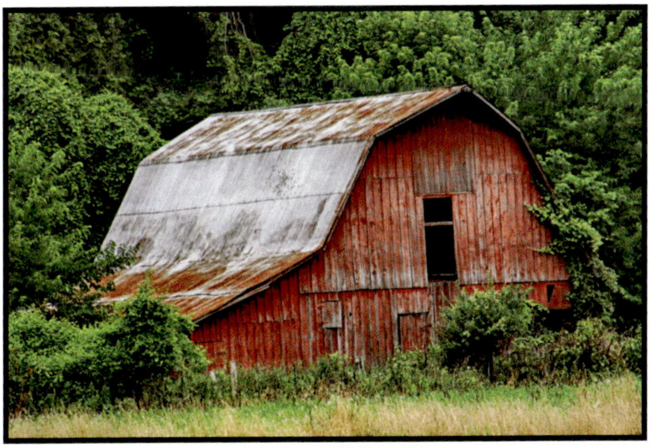

Old Barn off Hwy 79

For more information visit www.clarksvillemo.us

Illinois Destinations

All Within 150 Miles of Downtown St. Louis

EIGHTEEN

River Overlook

East St. Louis, Illinois (No Kidding!)

"*Whoa*" ... no one in their right mind goes driving in East St. Louis! While we don't "pack" (guns no; lunch sometimes) we are super careful about safety and we wouldn't send you to a place we thought was dangerous. This is such a great **scenic overlook** that we had to mention it. There are guards patrolling this area and while we wouldn't go at night the daytime is safe.

You can get such great photographs of the **Arch**, the **Old Courthouse**, and the **Eads Bridge** from this vantage point, and although we've never photographed **fireworks** from here, it has to be a good spot for that. Also, when the helicopter is taking tours, it flies right overhead. There are also the **barges**, **trains** and the Mississippi River.

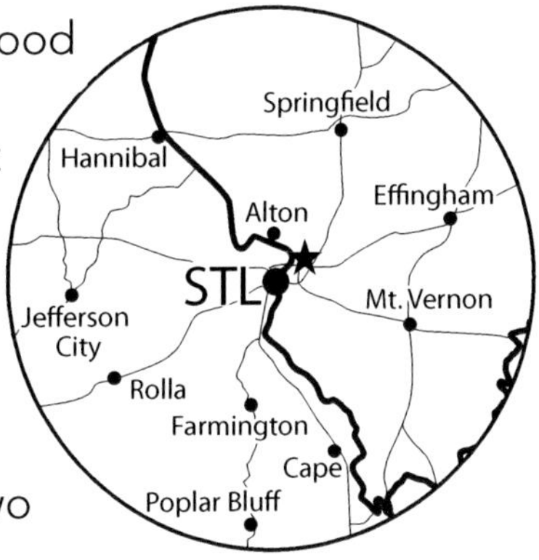

Approximate Mileage from downtown Downtown St. Louis: Two miles

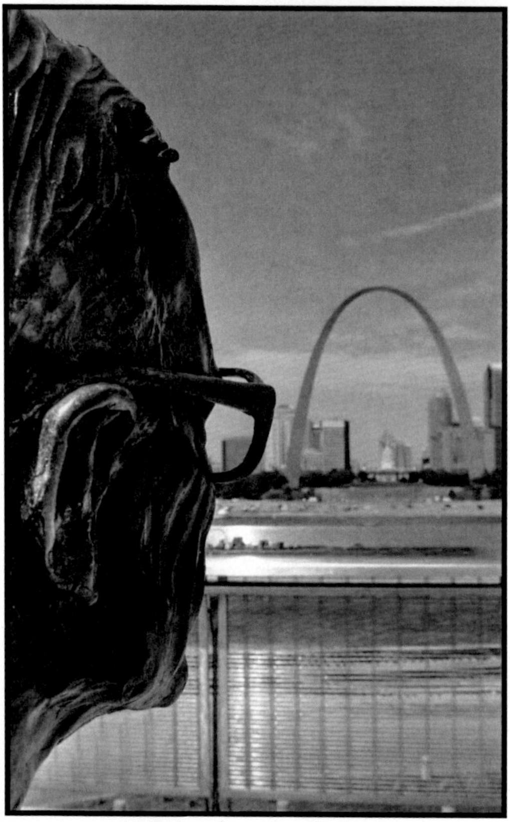

Arch View from East St. Louis.

Directions: Start out in downtown St. Louis. Go east on Market Street toward S. Tucker Blvd. Turn left onto N. Tucker Blvd. Turn right onto Washington Blvd, and this street will lead you right onto the Eads Bridge crossing into Illinois. At the end of the Bridge, make a sharp left turn onto River Park Drive, which takes you past the Casino Queen and along the Mississippi River. Drive past the Casino (which should be on your left) and you will see the Overlook. It is an open walkway with ramps. There is a parking lot right behind the Overlook.

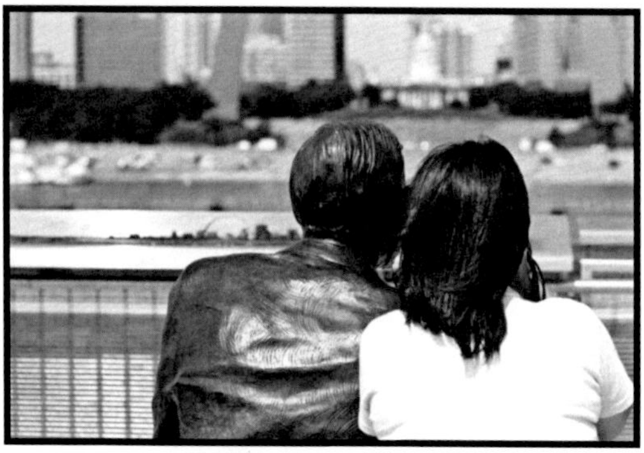

Bad Nancy and Friend.

Handicap Accessibility: Very good. While it is a little walk to the top of the Overlook it is all ramping and no stairs.

Food: If you don't eat at the Casino, go back the way you came and look for some place around the downtown area. Please don't drive around East St. Louis.

NINETEEN

Riverlands Migratory Bird Sanctuary

West Alton, Missouri and Alton, Illinois

If you like wildlife, this is an easy place to get to and loaded with all kinds of good photo ops. The Sanctuary encompasses a total of 3700 acres and within the Sanctuary is a 1200 acre **wetland/prairie** restoration project. There are roads available for driving or if you are especially energetic you can walk. This area hosts an abundant array of **waterfowl, shorebirds, swans, pelicans** (certain times of the year) and raptors to delight birdwatchers of all ages. January and February are especially busy with **eagle** watchers.

On the other side of Highway 67 (West Alton but still on the Missouri side) is another area that gives you a great view of Alton and the **bridge** going into Alton, along with more **water fowl**, including **Canvasback, Redhead, and Ring-necked ducks**.

The Riverlands Migratory Bird Sanctuary is listed on the National Audubon Society's Great River Birding Trail. There are several "indoor" buildings available for visiting also.

The website (www.riverlands.audubon.org) states that the trails are closed from October 15th through April 15th to foot traffic; however, cars are allowed on the roads. We've been there many times, including January and February, and we aren't BIG hikers. We fear you might freeze to death walking during those months since fierce winds blow off the Mighty Mississippi.

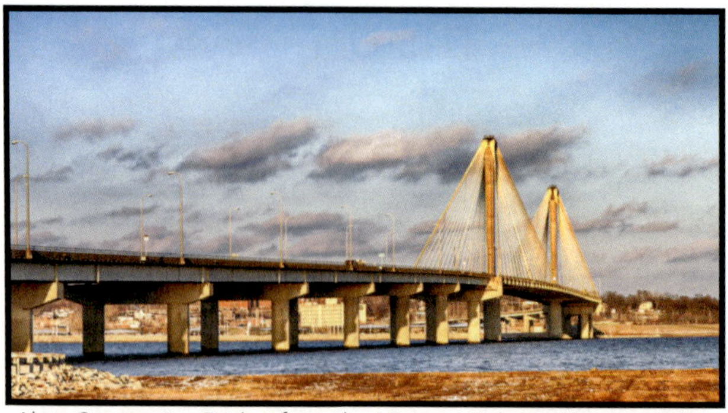

Alton Suspension Bridge from the Missouri Side Looking into Alton

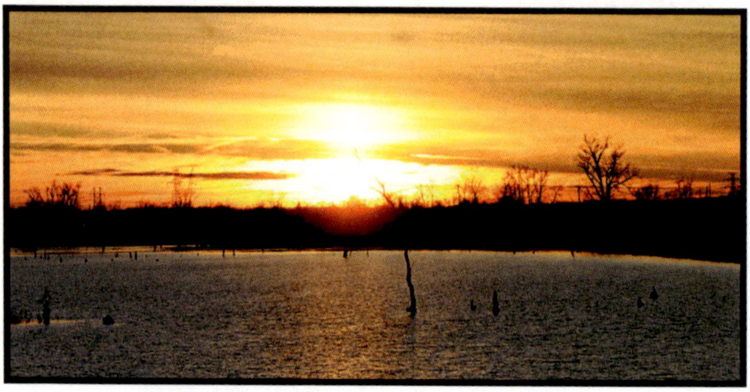

Wetlands Across 67 on the Missouri Side

You will get some great shots of not only the bridge, but the Melvin Price **Locks and Dam**.

Directions: Riverlands Migratory Bird Sanctuary is just a 30 minute drive from downtown. Take 70 West of downtown and stay on this until you pass Lambert International Airport (on your right). Start looking for signs to 270 North and take 270 until you reach Highway 367 North. 367 will take you across the Missouri River and there 367 is called Highway 67. Go figure. In about 4 miles you will start noticing very flat land. Look for the second gas station on your right – Phillip's 66. Turn in and you are there.

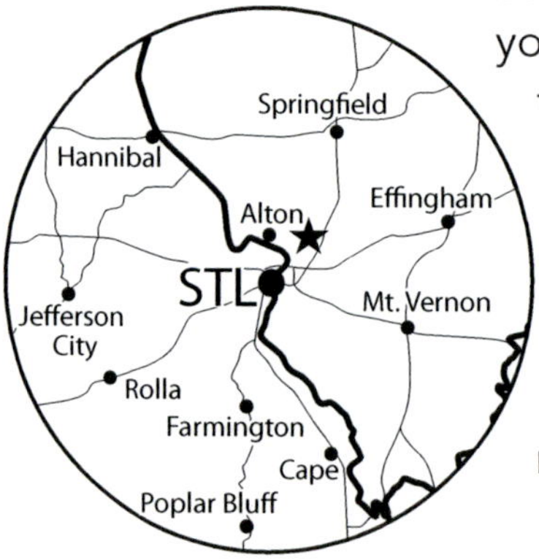

There are other routes from downtown but if you aren't familiar with the City, I would stick to the main highways I mentioned above.

Approximate Mileage from Downtown St. Louis: 30 miles.

Handicap Accessibility: Excellent.

Food: Plenty of picnic areas, but if you didn't bring anything, you can always hit the gas station for Slim Jims and Doritos! Otherwise, drive into Alton.

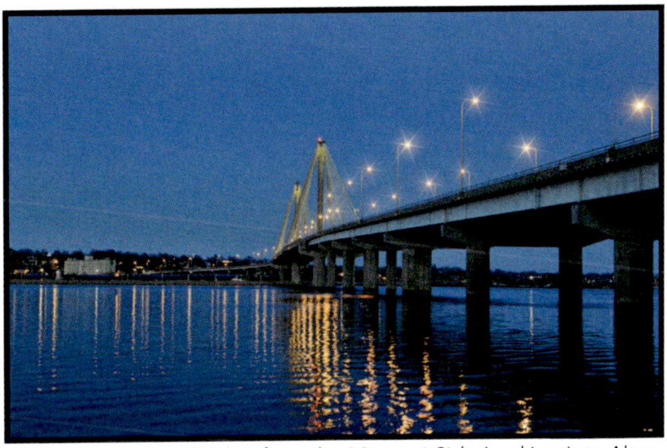

Alton Suspension Bridge from the Missouri Side Looking into Alton

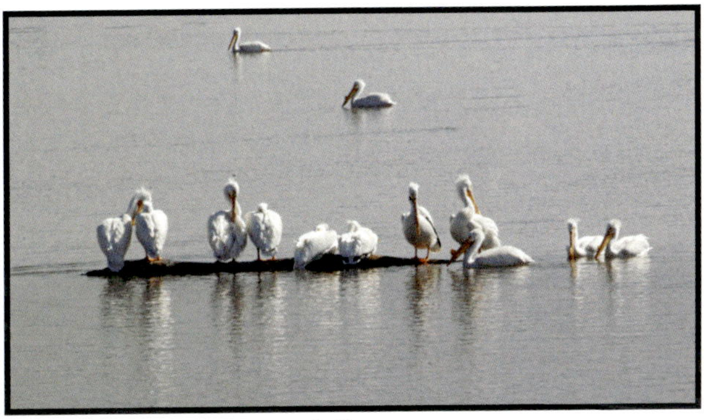

Pelicans

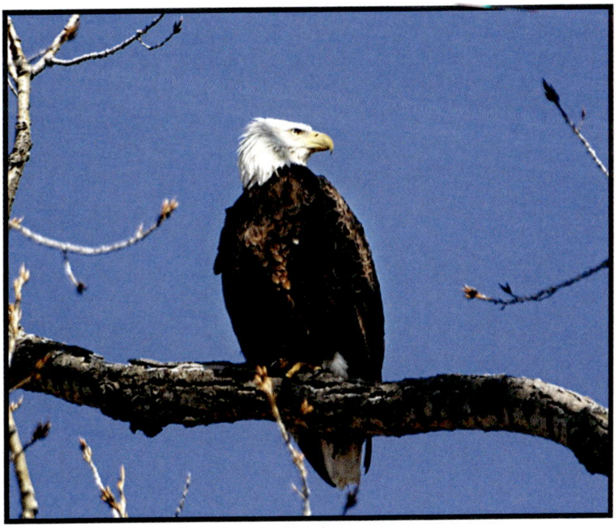

Eagle

TWENTY

Grafton, Illinois

Grafton is a little **river town** right outside of Alton, Illinois and we mention this because we can't quite get it together to go to Maine and we LOVE **lighthouses**. So the next best thing is here in Grafton. While it's not the Atlantic Ocean, it IS the **Mississippi River** and not only will you see the **lighthouse**, the last time we were there **seagulls** started swarming (do birds "swarm"?) our car. It was quite thrilling as we saw ourselves as Tippi Hedrun in Alfred Hitchcock's "The Birds." Well, we do have big imaginations! If you are brave you can throw crackers or bread and you will have more seagulls than you can count.

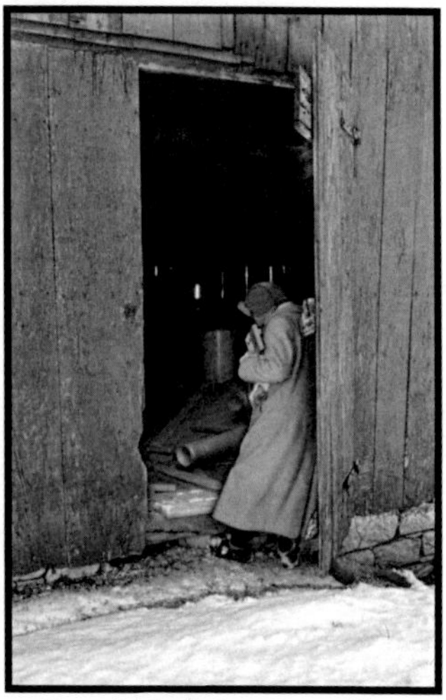

Cowgirl Judy in a Barn Along the Great River Road

Grafton is also home to one of our favorite restaurants – The Fin Inn. We had to mention this one because where else can you have lunch next to **HUGE catfish**, **HUGE turtles** and whatever else inhabits the Mississippi River? Seriously, every booth has a gigantic **aquarium** right there next to you and the fish love to watch you eat. We've all had some strange love-life stories but Nancy had a catfish fall in love with her and he never moved the whole time we were there. He just kept puckering and re-puckering up his lips and staring at her. Oh, we should mention that your lunch does not come out of the aquariums, at least they don't fish in front of you. Ignorance can be bliss. By the way, we've always had very good food there!

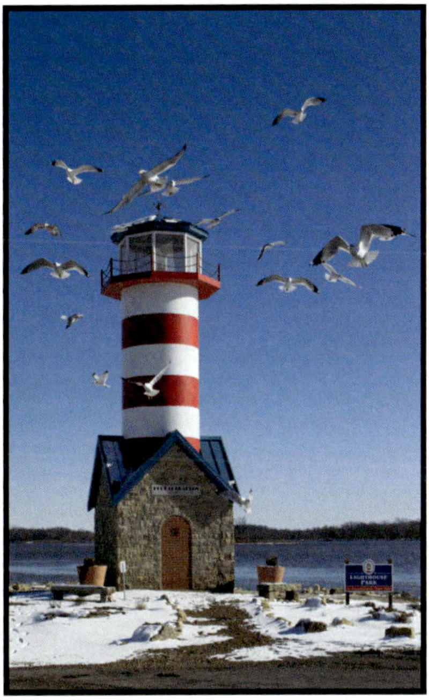
Lighthouse

There are many other photo ops in town including **old buildings** and a few interesting, **older homes**, along with **antique stores** and general geegaws interspersed here and there.

Approximate mileage from Downtown St. Louis: 30 miles

Directions to Grafton: From downtown take 70 West and stay on this until you pass Lambert International Airport (on your right). Start looking for signs to 270 North and take 270 North until you reach Highway 367 North. 367 will take you across the Missouri River and then 367 becomes Highway 67. Go figure. Cross over the Alton suspension bridge into Alton and make your first left at the end of the bridge. Stay on this road until you see the Casino on your left and a stop light.

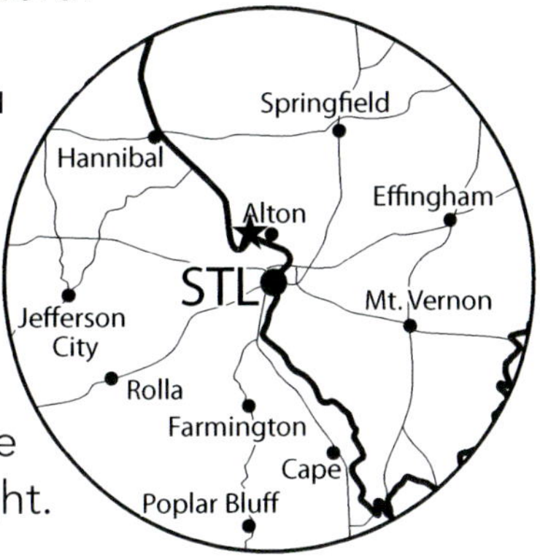

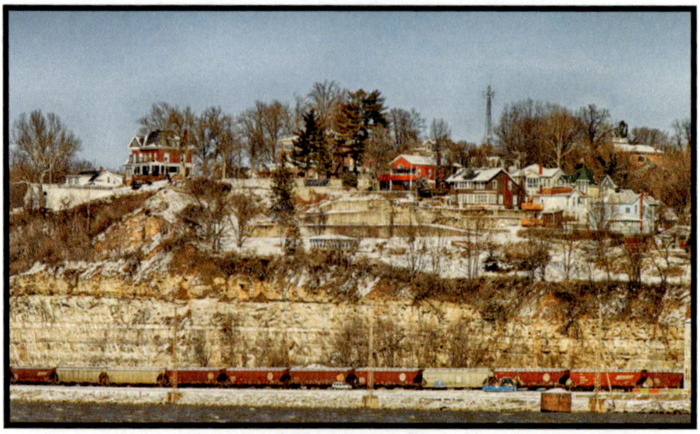

Alton and The Great River Road

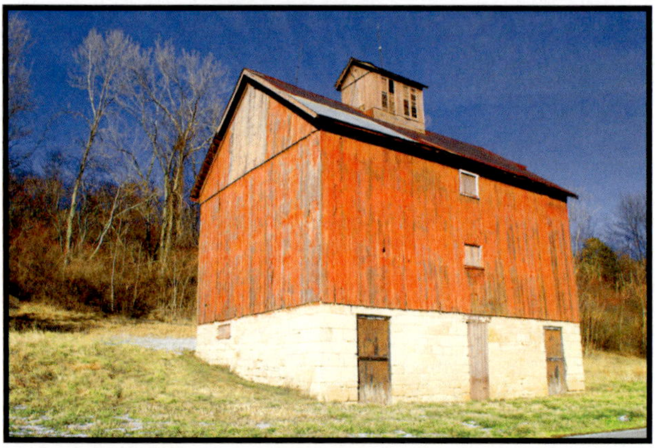

Barn Along The Great River Road

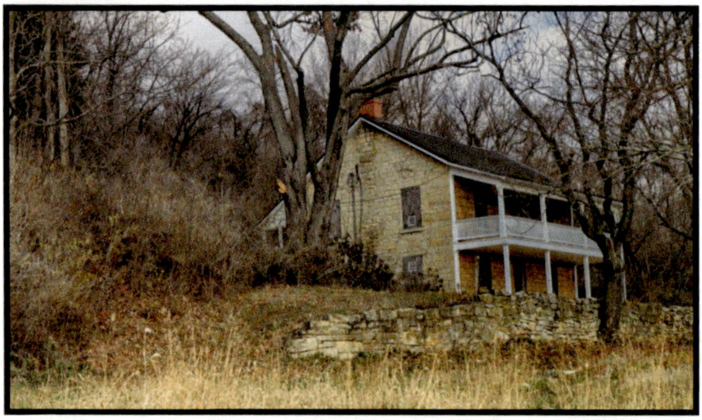

Limestone Farm House Along The Great River Road

Turn left onto Hwy 100 – **The Great River Road**. You will come to Grafton in approximately 6 miles. Once in Grafton, take a left on Vine Street and you can't miss the **lighthouse.**

The **Fin Inn** is located at 1500 West Main Street, Grafton, IL 62037 (618-786-2030) and sits back off the main road on your right, as you head north up The Great River Road.

Handicap Accessibility: Very good as it is very flat around the lighthouse. The restaurant has a paved ramp up a small hill.

Food: The Fin Inn is our recommendation (see paragraph on pages 100-101).

TWENTY~ONE

Elsah, Illinois

This **quaint little town** is right outside of Alton, Illinois, down **The Great River Road**. There are lots of sights along this fabulous Road so allow plenty of time. Here are a few things to look for: **lighthouse** (Grafton), **old barn** with **stone foundation** and house to match (on the Sam Vadalabene Bike Trail), and **The Golden Eagle Ferry**. This is a popular place for **eagle watching** in January and February.

The little town of Elsah was founded in 1853 and has a population of 672. As soon as you turn off the Great River Road (directions at the end of this chapter) you will enter the town and experience the Twilight Zone (do do do do, do do do do) ... you've gone back in time. There are only 2 main streets so park your car and take a walk, or you can drive through the town. People are very friendly here and I suppose used to tourists, although I've been here many times over the last 40+ years and I've never really seen anything close to "big crowds," which is nice because I like to pretend I live here. So far, I've resisted going up on people's porches and helping myself to a sit-down in a wicker rocking chair or porch swing.

There are several **churches** and **houses** built long ago by **stone masons** who lived here. One interesting house even has an **antique gas pump** in front; there is a **creek** running through town, along with **foot bridges**, **a park**, well tended lawns and flower beds. You will keep looking for Sheriff Andy Taylor driving around or Aunt Bea with a basket full of fried chicken heading to a church picnic. There are also **picket fences**, along with **little stone walls**. We are telling you – this place is unbelievable.

While we are not big fans of **museums**, this one is a must see. It's housed in an **old school house** on LaSalle Street and while it's free, they appreciate a donation We were allowed to shoot pictures and had a great deal of fun (look for the **old piano**, **sewing machine and antiques galore**). There is very good lighting inside and we used tripods. The museum is open April through October, Saturday and Sunday 1-4 pm.

Approximate mileage from Downtown St. Louis: 30 miles

Directions: From downtown, get on 70 North and take this all the way out to 270 North to Highway 373. Go north on 373 across the Alton Bridge. Take a left at the end of the bridge and this road will lead you (you will be south of the Alton downtown area – great antique stores) onto Highway 100, which is also known as **The Great River Road**. Follow the River Road about 10 miles and Elsah will be on your right. The Mississippi River is on your left. Weren't the town fathers smart in naming this the Great River Road?? There is only one little sign for Elsah so be on the lookout. It's easy to pass up.

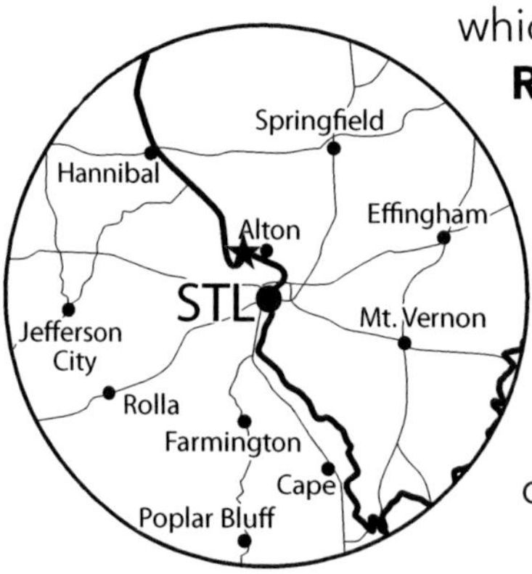

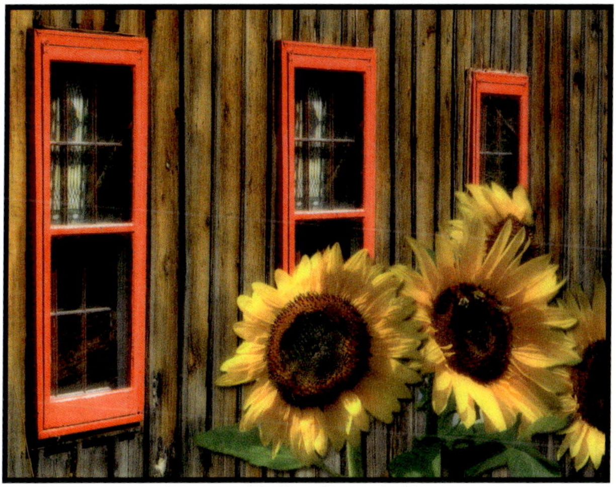

House with Gas Pump in Front

Handicap Accessibility: We would say good since Elsah is pretty flat and there are a few sidewalks, plus you can see all from a car window.

Food: There is a small restaurant in town with yummy looking desserts and you can get bottled water or something cold to drink. A very cozy little place.

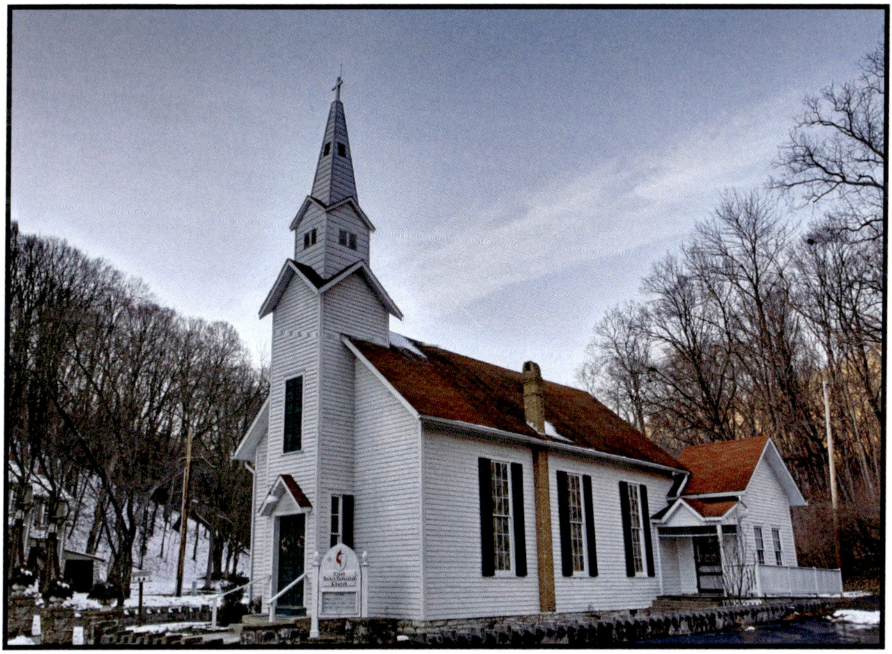

Church in Elsah

TWENTY~TWO

Principia College

Elsah, Illinois

While you are in Elsah, you must take the road up to this **gorgeous college campus**. It is called a School and College for Christian Scientists. The directions are listed below.

At the main entrance you have to stop at the Guard Gate to get a visitor sign for your car. Be sure to ask if it is all right for you to go inside **the Church**. The Guard will tell you if there are services being conducted and whether you may enter or not. The road around the campus is one-way so you just follow it around. About mid-way through your tour you will come upon the Church. What a **scenic view from this bluff**! We entered the Church and immediately went into our "inside voices." It is beautiful in its simplicity and we had the place all to ourselves so we took plenty of shots. There is also a balcony with an **old Organ**.

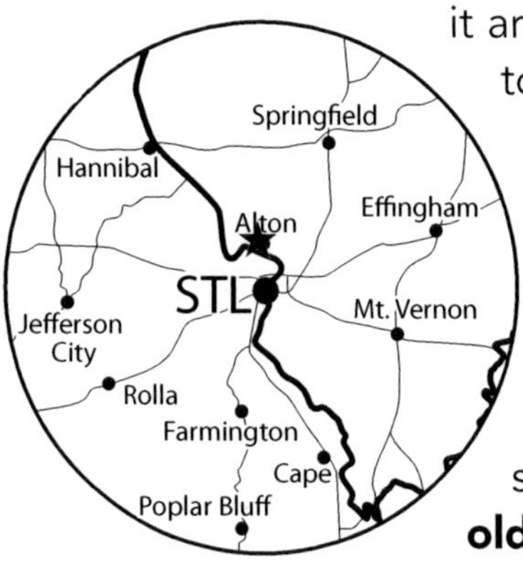

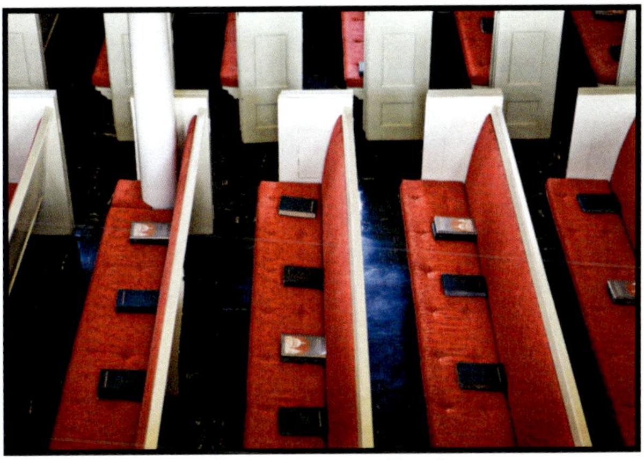
Christian Science Church

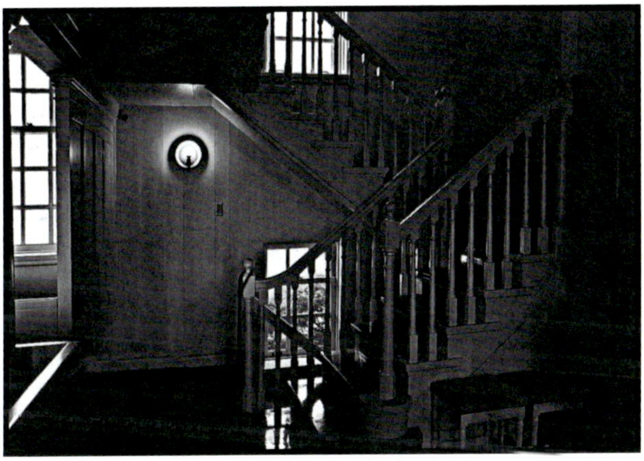
Church Vestibule

Approximate Mileage from Downtown St. Louis:
30 miles

Directions:
Principia College campus is open for visits and tours Monday-Saturday: 10 am-Sunset. Sunday: Noon-Sunset.
Principia College is located in **Elsah**, Illinois, 12 miles north of Alton, off the Great River Road, Route 100. To reach the campus entrance, turn right at Elsah Road, bearing right to Mill Street. Go halfway through the village of Elsah to the first stop sign. Turn right and go up the hill. If using GPS, the coordinates for the gatehouse are: Latitude: 38.9555, Longitude: -90.3475

Food: There is nothing on the campus.

Handicap Accessibility: Excellent. You can park your car very close to the Church and there are a few steps up into the building.

TWENTY~THREE

Alto Pass, Illinois

There are many Photo Ops in and around this area and it's a good day trip, especially during warm weather because of all the **wineries** and **fruit orchards**. You will also be in the **Shawnee National Forest**. For those of you not in the habit of hanging around Southern Illinois, the land becomes extremely hilly with big **limestone formations**. If we had stopped at every winery we passed we would still be trying to sober up. **Beautiful country, wine, fruit, scenic vistas** … who could ask for more?

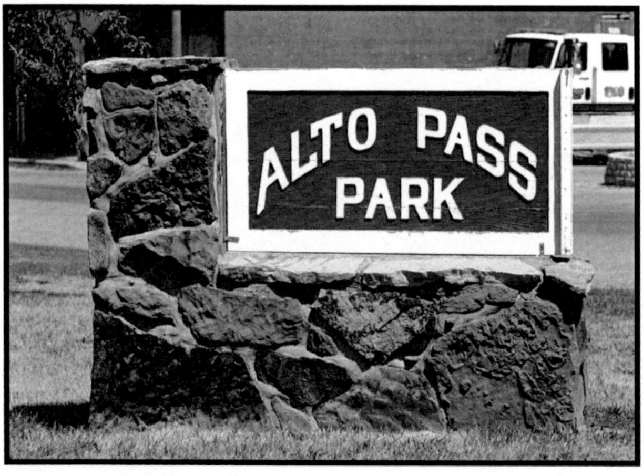

Photo Op #1
Alto Pass

This is a **quaint little town** with a variety of places to shoot (or not). There is a **log cabin** and plenty of **older**

buildings. Our favorite is a place called **The Root Beer Saloon** which is located right in the center of town. Note: The owner of the Root Beer Saloon will NOT allow you to take photos inside the actual Saloon/restaurant, but he's very talkative and you can take all the photos you want outside. His name is "Mike" and he is also a **guitar** maker. When we went outside, Mike offered to show us his workshop next door and gave us a tour of that building AND he showed us a guitar he had just finished. He was more than generous in allowing us to take pictures. However, they do NOT take credit cards in the Saloon so you will need cash if you want the famous "Root Beer Float." Who would drive all that way and not partake?

Photo Ops #2
Bald Knob

Bald Knob, located just down the road from Alto Pass, is the home of outstanding **scenic views** and a **HUGE white cross** that can be seen for miles. Visit website www.baldknowcross.com. We were there mid-day (isn't that the way it always works because the sun is usually too bright to take good photographs) and decided we must go back in the fall, around sunset. It is such a **superb vista**!

Photo Op #3
Makanda

A small, but **old,** little **town**. This place is on the way to Giant City State Park. It's a fun little setting with a few **great old buildings** and **houses** and a store that has fun **jewelry and crafts** made by local people.

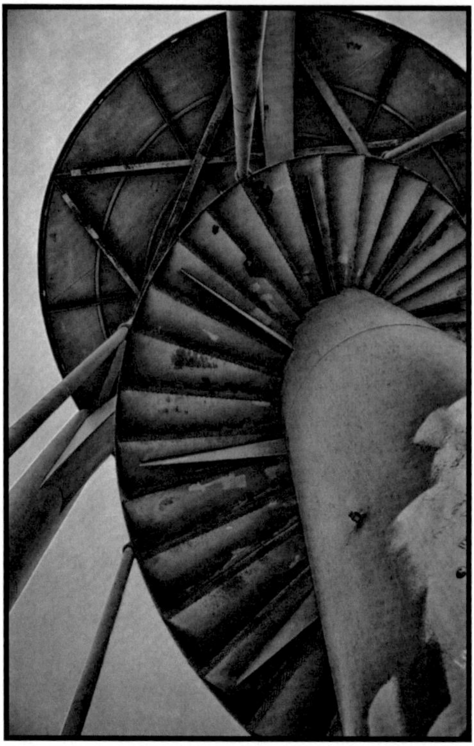
Water Tower

Photo Op #4
Giant City State Park

This park is famous for **its gigantic rock formations** and **beautiful creeks, vistas**, etc. Be sure to take the road up to the **lodge and water tower.** We didn't eat in the Lodge but the restaurant looked lovely (constructed with wood and beams with gorgeous **stairwells**) and full of people on a Sunday afternoon.

Photo Op #5
Water Tower

Up by the **lodge** is a huge **water tower** (hard to miss). We were there on one of the hottest days of the summer and since I had just had my hip replaced (good excuse, huh?) we didn't climb to the top but the stairs and Tower provide plenty of **curves** and **angles** to shoot from below.

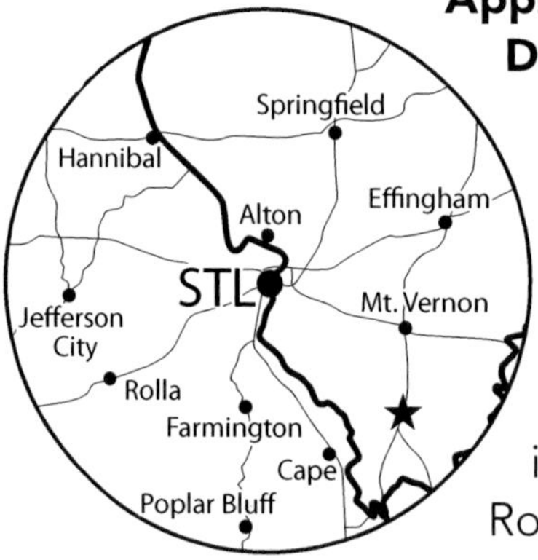

Approximate Mileage from Downtown St. Louis: 111 miles

Directions: Take 270 South, across the Jefferson Barracks Bridge and then take the exit to Columbia, which takes you south on Route 3. Follow Route 3 South all the way into Red Bud, Illinois. We then took Route 154 out of Red Bud and you will go through the following little towns: Baldwin, Sparta and Pinckneyville. In Pinckneyville we took 127 South toward Carbondale. You will be entering the **Shawnee National Forest**. Stay on Route 127 (it winds around a lot) until you come to signs for Alto Pass. The four Photo Ops we mentioned are all within a 10-15 mile radius of Alto Pass.

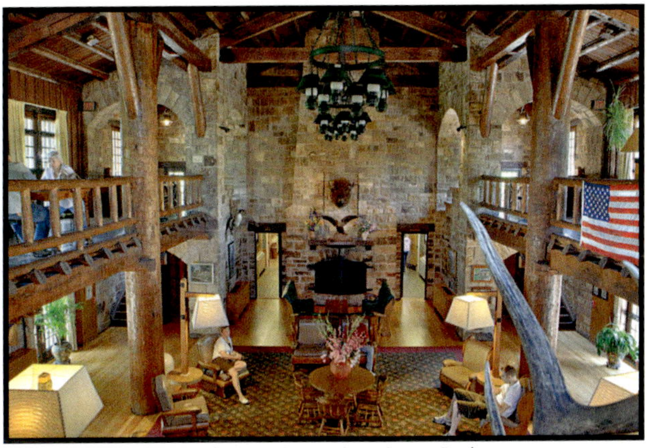

Lodge at Giant City State Park

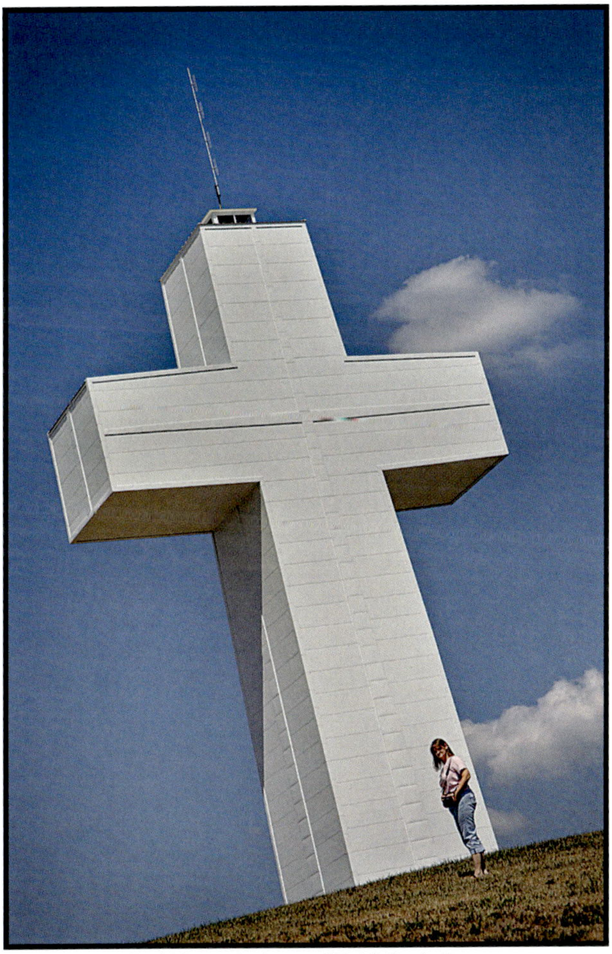

Bad Nancy in front of Bald Knob Cross

Food: Besides all the wineries, we recommend The Root Beer Saloon in Alto Pass; or go on to Giant City State Park and eat at the lodge inside the park.

Handicap Accessibility: Moderate due to

lots of walking. Alto Pass is fairly flat. You can drive up to the Bald Knob Cross and observe the vistas from the car. Makanda is also in a flat place. Giant City State Park does have a ramp for entrance into the restaurant.

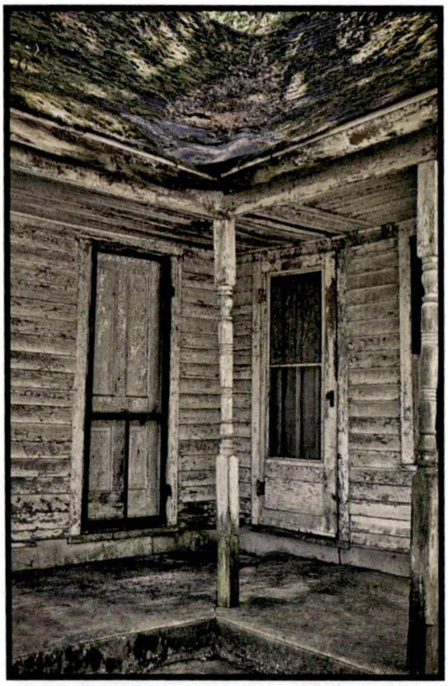

Old House in Makanda

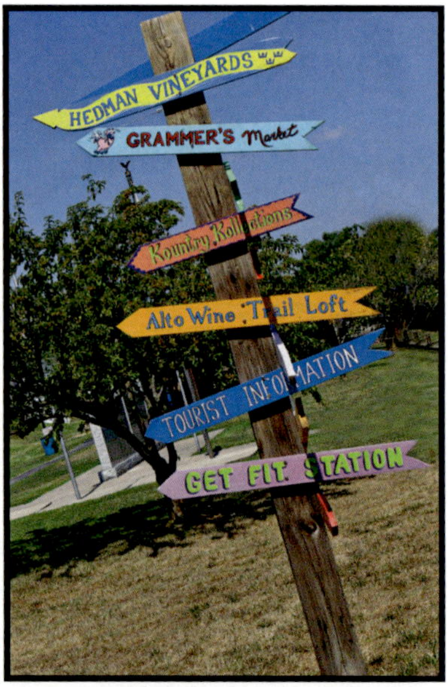

Alto Pass

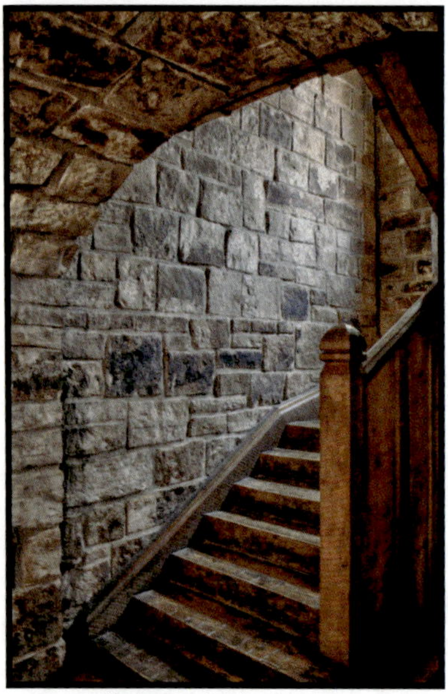

Staircase in the Lodge

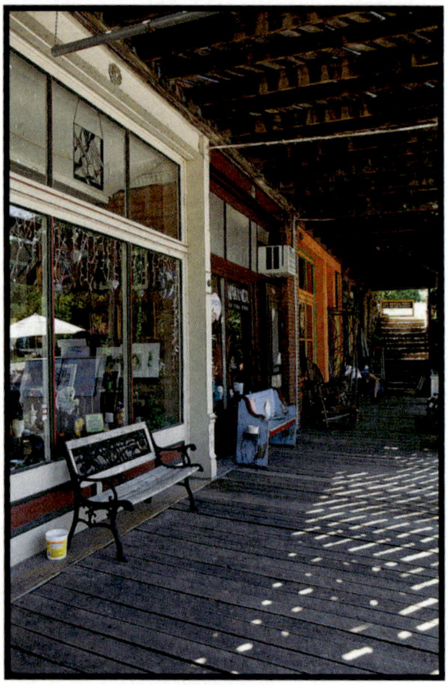

Makanda

TWENTY~FOUR

Maeystown, Illinois

Maeystown is another charming, **quaint little town** that was settled by German immigrants around 1852. This village is full of **scenic views**, having been built in a **valley** along side a **creek**. Sixty **significant buildings** still exist, including the original **stone church**, the **stone bridge**, Zeitinger's **Mill**, various **outbuildings**, **barns** and **smokehouses** made of **limestone**, **brick** and **wood**. There's also an **antique** shop or two.

The town is quite hilly but that just adds to the charm. Stop in the **General Store** or hit up one of the local coffee shops. Check out the following website because this town has quite a few annual events including a Springfest, Oktoberfest, Christmas and one of those German Pancake and Sausage dinners: www.maeystown.com.

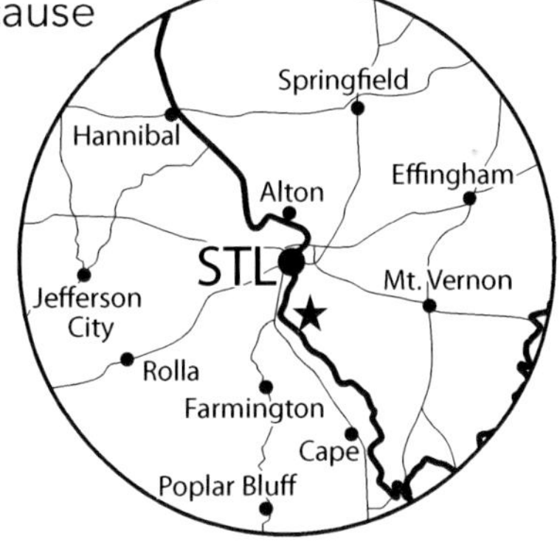

Approximate Mileage from Downtown St. Louis: 40 miles

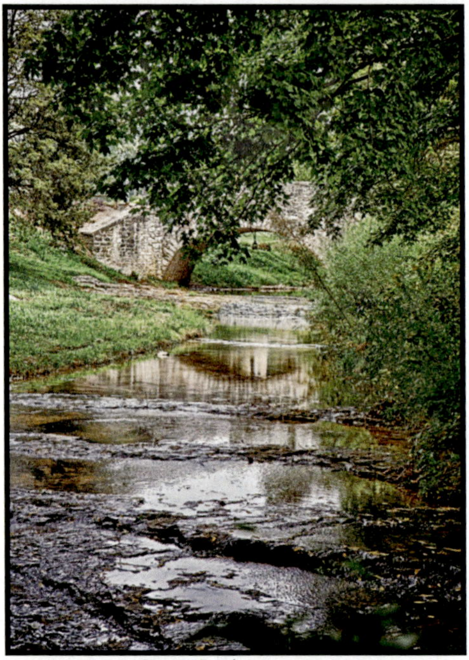
Stone Bridge in town

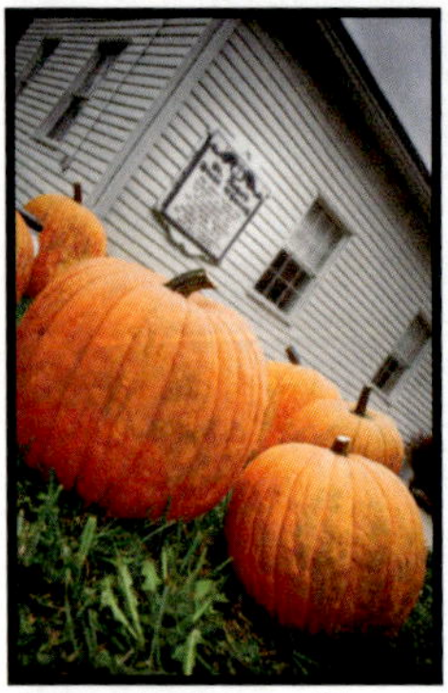
Pumpkin Fest at Church

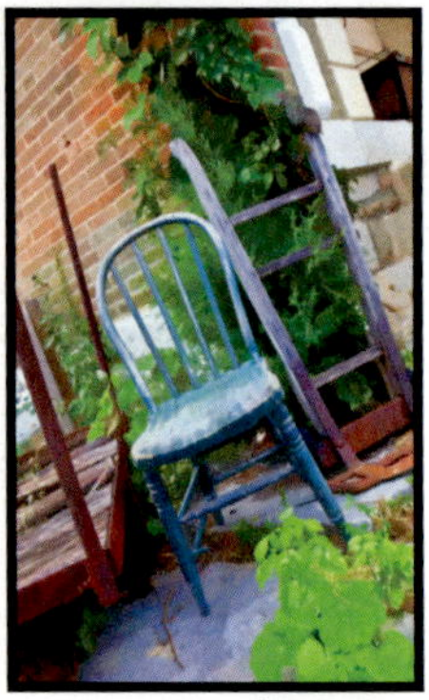
Antique Store

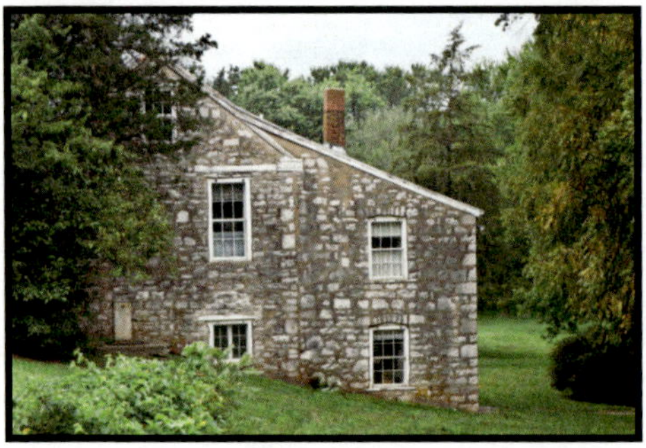
Guest House

Directions: FROM St. Louis and points north and west. Take I-55 South to I-255 East. Take I-255 East to IL-3 South. Take IL-3 South to IL-156 in Waterloo. Take IL-156 West one block to Lakeview Drive. Take Lakeview Drive (changes into Maeystown Road) to Maeystown

FROM central Illinois and points north and east. Take I-55 south to I-255. Take I-255 South to IL-3 South. Take IL-3 South to IL-156 in Waterloo. Take IL-156 West one block to Lakeview Drive. Take Lakeview Drive (changes into Maeystown Road) to Maeystown.

Food: We were there during a wet, cold fall weekend and the only thing open (besides the General Store) was the coffee house. Be sure to check dates and find out what's open before you head that way.

Handicap Accessibility: Walking is moderate due to all the hills in town, but you can see everything from a car window.

TWENTY~FIVE

Prairie du Rocher and Chester, Illinois

There are so many photo ops in this area that we want to tell you about. Actually, if you read the write-up on Maeystown (now we are testing you) in the previous chapter, you are so close to these other treasures.

We know you are dying to know what Prairie du Rocher means. This translates to "prairie by the rock." Now you can WOW your friends and family.

Photo Op #1
Deserted Mining Structure

(GPS Coordinates: +38° 6' 7.88", -90° 6' 48.63")

As you are about two miles North of Prairie du Rocher, traveling south start looking to your left (the **Mississippi River** is on your far right). You will be on a road named Bluff Road and there is a reason for this. Yep, you guessed it. To your left are huge **limestone bluffs**. Isn't that absolutely amazing? Our forefathers may not have been wildly creative but at least they made some sense.

This amazing, **three story silo/plant/mining structure** looking thing pops up out of the trees and is built into the side of a rock bluff. Check out the picture – and notice Angie standing among the trees. This structure is BIG. We think this was part of a rock quarry or mining operation for what else? **Limestone**. We are so astute. The address is 7965 Bluff Rd.

There is a gravel parking lot of sorts practically right in front so to us that just invited exploration. We sent in "The Fearless Angie" first who went tromping off into the woods to see if there was any way to enter this building. B.N. and I parked the car and then took the short trek back to the woods to see if we could find Angie. At this point we discovered another, closer place to park so as we were heading back to the car to move it closer, a big, noisy, heavy clomping sound came from the woods. We knew it wasn't Angie because she was further up the hill and over to our left. B.N. (while she will face up to any human, has a *real* fear of anything on four legs) screams "BEAR" and that was all it took for us to make a mad dash toward the car. I have to admit that at our age "mad dash" is an oxymoron because running of any kind makes us laugh so hard the tears run down our legs. I know, too much information. But we just wanted to give you the picture that B.N. and I were REALLY scared. We jumped into the car and started to peel out of there when we realized that we were leaving Angie behind. Oops.

Deciding our scary noise was only a deer, Angie persuaded us to get out of the car and make a short little climb up the hill so we could look into this structure and it was more than worth the climb: Great **peeling paint, rust,** an **old light structure** and lots of natural lighting. Whoopee!

Photo Op #2
Fort de Chartres
Outside Prairie du Rocher, Illinois

There have been three **forts** in this place, the original fort was a wooden stockade built in 1718. The second fort was lost during floods from the Mississippi River and the last was completed in 1760 from **limestone** quarried in Prairie du Rocher. For more information visit www.greatriverroad.com or Visitors Guide to Prairie du Rocher.

Photo Op #3
Mary's River Covered Bridge
(GPS Coordinates: N 37° 56.885' W 89° 45.974')
Outside of Chester, Illinois

This is located a little further down the road from Prairie du Rocher and is worth the drive to Chester. See directions below. This **covered bridge** has been well kept and as you can see we had fun taking photos and experimenting with our off-camera flashes.

Here's another little bit of trivia. Chester is known as the "Home of Popeye" because Elzie C. Segar, the creator of Popeye, was born in Chester and many of the Popeye characters were modeled after real residents of Chester!

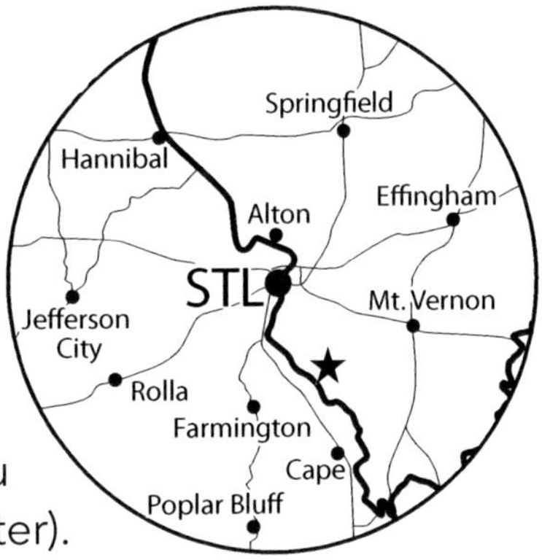

Approximate Mileage from Downtown St. Louis to Prairie du Rocher: 50 miles

Approximate Mileage from Prairie du Rocher to Chester: 22 miles

Directions: We are going to take you from **Maeystown** (the previous chapter).

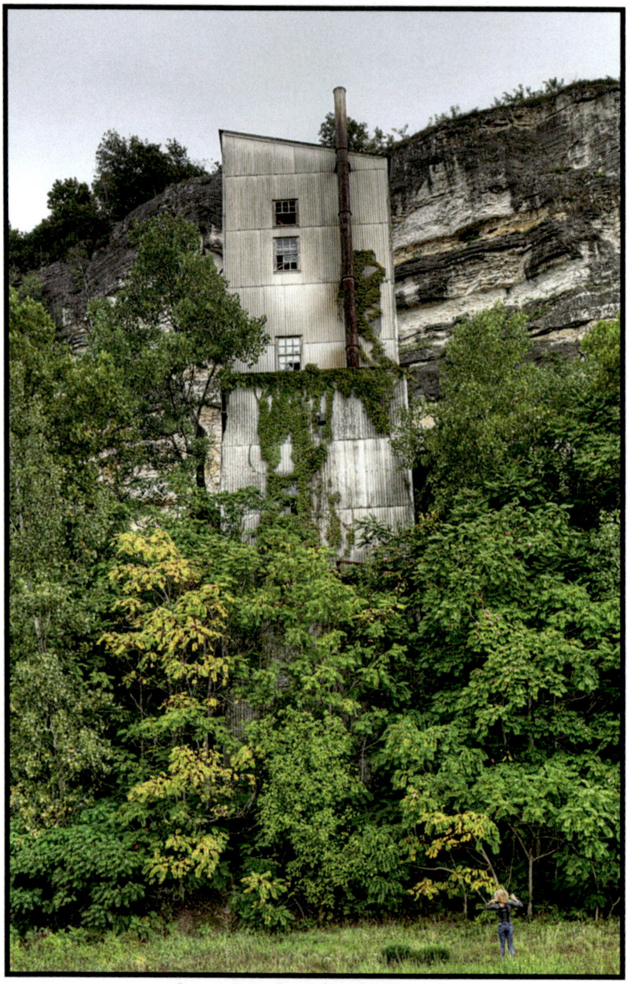

See Angie Standing in Corner

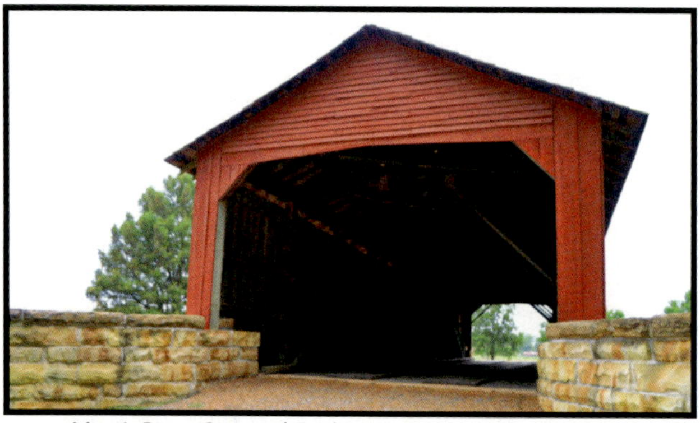

Mary's River Covered Bridge Outside Chester, Illinois

There are many routes to take if you look on the map, however, we took Route 3 out of Maeystown to Bluff Road and followed it south to **Prairie du Rocher**. From Prairie du Rocher, we followed Bluff Road South to Route 3 and took this into **Chester**. Once in Chester you want State Street or Route 150, which will take you to Mary's River Covered Bridge. This is about 8 miles out of Chester and the Bridge will be on your right.

To go home, we took the Bridge in Chester (crossing the Mississippi River) into Perryville and took Highway 55 home.

Handicap Accessibility: Good for **Photo Op #1** – the three-story silo/plant/mining structure. The road is perfectly flat and you can photograph from the road/car without having to climb up to peer into this deserted building; Good for **Photo Op #2** because the ground is flat; Good for **Photo Op #3** because you can drive right up to the bridge. There is a short ramp onto the bridge.

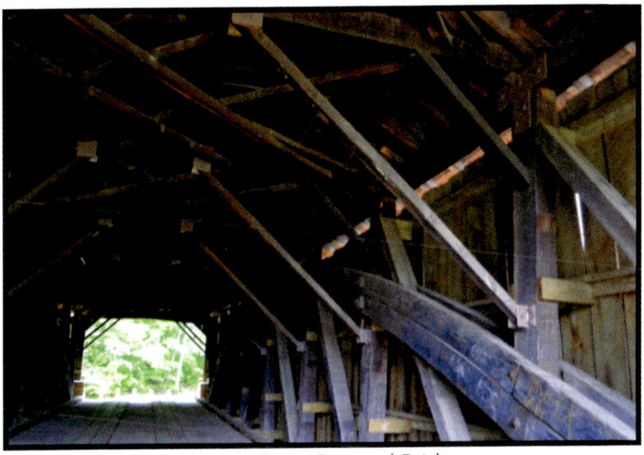

Mary's River Covered Bridge

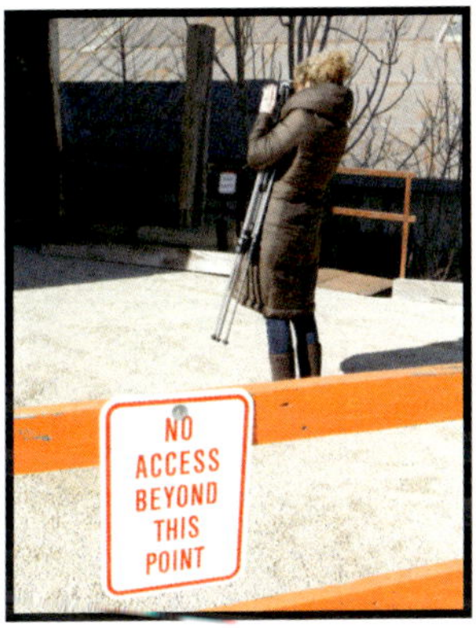

Fearless Angie

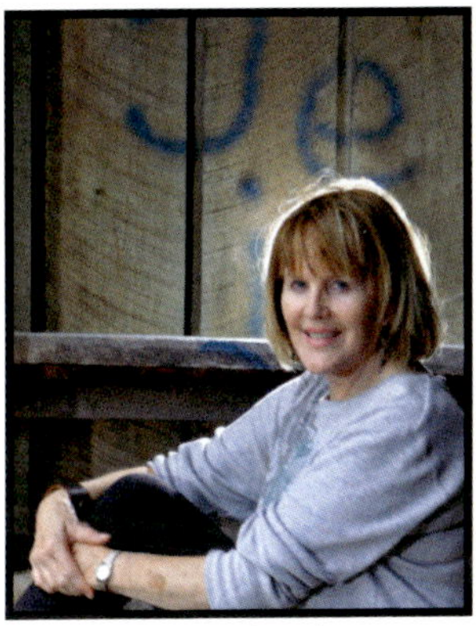

Cowgirl Judy

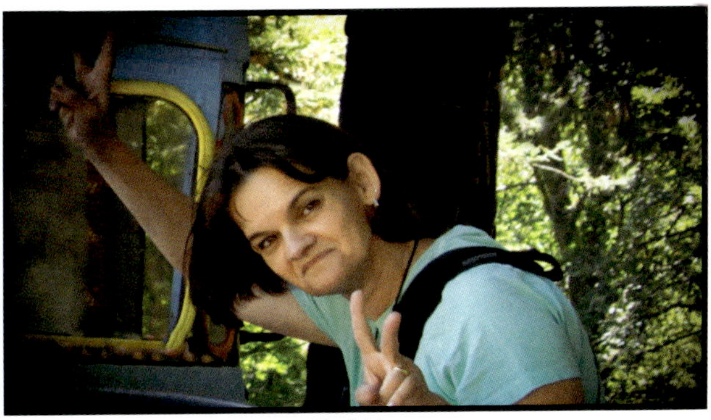

Bad Nancy

Food: We ate at Lisa's in Prairie du Rocher, which is located in an old, **old building**. The food was very good and the place has lots of historical photographs.

TWENTY~SIX

Arthur, Illinois and Rockome Gardens

The first place Nancy and I ever visited on a bonafide, **overnight "road trip"** was into Amish Country. While there are other locations where you can find the Amish, we picked Arthur since a friend of Nancy's had been there and it sounded like an all inclusive place with tons of photo ops. And, it is.

The Amish are very private people and as photographers we feel we had a responsibility to respect their main wish of not having their faces photographed, which has to do with their religious beliefs. We tried to respect that; yet, we feel like we still got some fun photographs of **buggies**, **horses**, the backs of people, **bicycles**, etc. Their **farmland** is absolutely gorgeous and immaculately kept so you will get lots of **scenics**, too.

Nancy had never seen any Amish people before so she was terribly excited. Upon seeing our first horse and buggy, Nancy started shouting, "There they are! OMG, they are everywhere!" We must have pulled our car over a hundred times waiting for the buggies to pass us so we could jump out of the car and

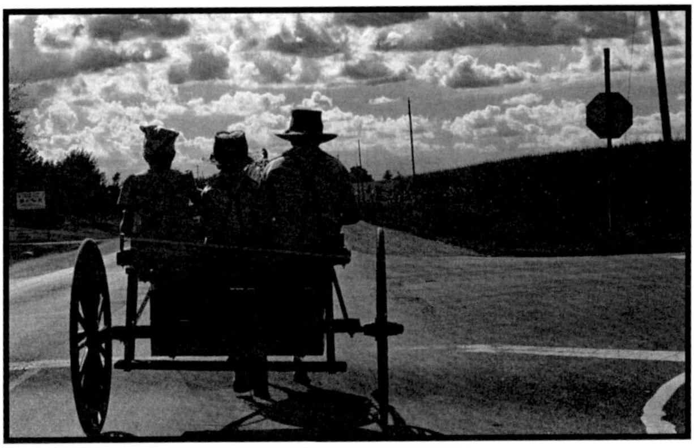

Amish Children in Buggy

shoot their backs. (Like the Amish didn't know what we were doing.)

When you get into Arthur, you will pass a Dollar General Store, and there is sure to be a couple of buggies tied up in the parking lot. Your next stop should be in the middle of town at a place called The Woodloft (1-888-321-9663). The address is 138 S. Vine, Arthur, Il 61911. This place rents CD's that will take you on a tour of **local farms** and explain their history and customs. It's well worth the $10 rental to pop this CD in your car and take off. We kept the CD for 2 days and revisited a lot of these farms to catch different lighting/weather. You will also see people working in their **gardens**, hanging out **wash**, and using **horses to plow** and/or harvest crops. Also, there are lots and lots of **barns** on beautiful **country roads**.

The town of Arthur itself is a fun place just to walk around and visit the **antique shops**, **restaurants** and **bakeries**. There are lots of Amish on their **bikes** as well as **horse and buggies**. Simply fascinating and **scenic**.

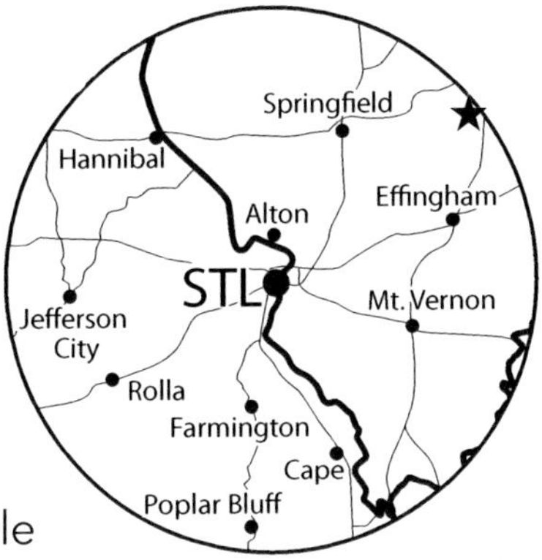

Sunday is Church Day and the Amish meet for services at each other's homes. If you get up early and hit the country roads, you will see many buggies and people

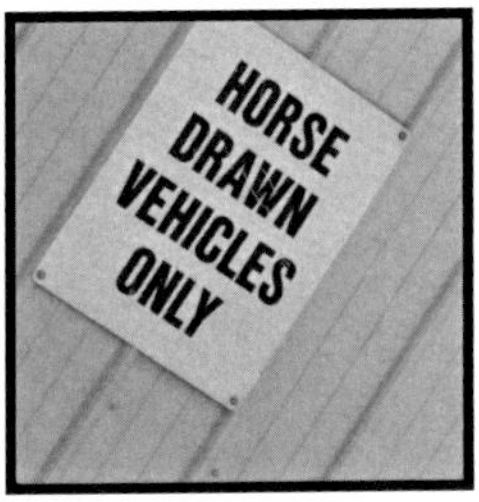

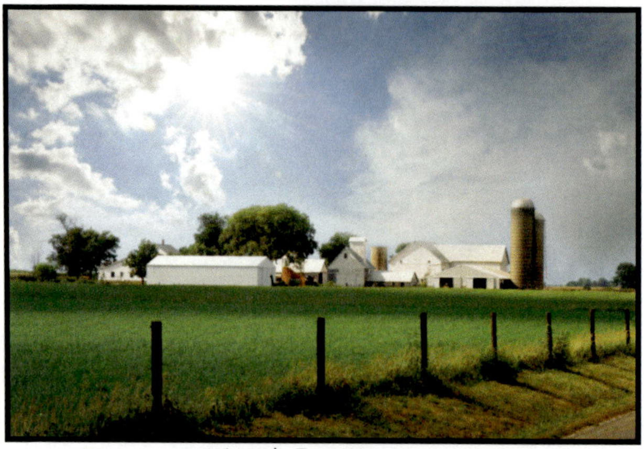

Amish Farm House

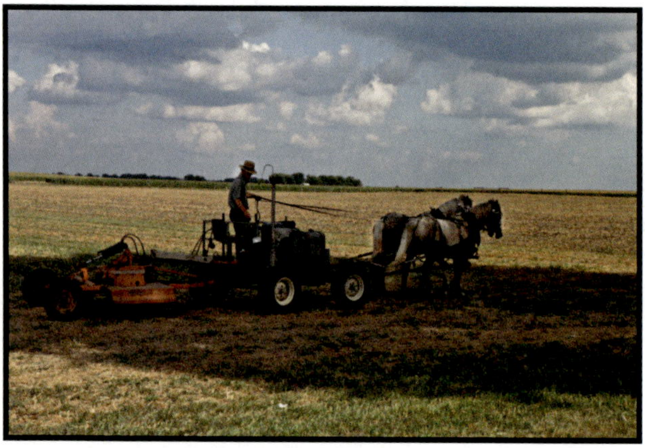

Farming a Field with Horses

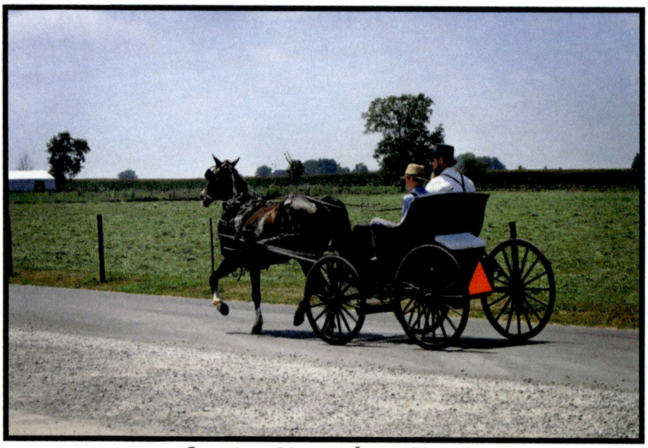

Coming Home from Town

walking, heading toward someone's house. HINT: Nancy discovered that on Saturday if you see a long, gray or dark green wagon parked in someone's yard, that is more than likely where the church services will be held since the wagons hold the benches that are taken into houses for the parishioners.

We respected their privacy and stayed out of the way, but who could resist taking a shot of the **line of buggies** parked outside during their service?

If you love fresh baked goods, you must stop at Beachy's Bulk

Food, 259 N. County Road 200E, 217-543-3447, which is on the CD tour. If a store has a sign outside, it means we, the English, are welcome to enter. There were gigantic cinnamon rolls, about the size of a normal cake, waiting for us. Did I mention they were iced and freshly baked that morning? Nancy and I split one (although we could have each eaten a whole one). We sat in the car outside and wolfed it down using our fingers. Delicious! We were so busy eating that we nearly missed several horse and buggies driving past us. We lamented many times over the fact that we didn't buy a case of cinnamon rolls and take them home. Ha. Like they would have made it home. But, then, there were the pies

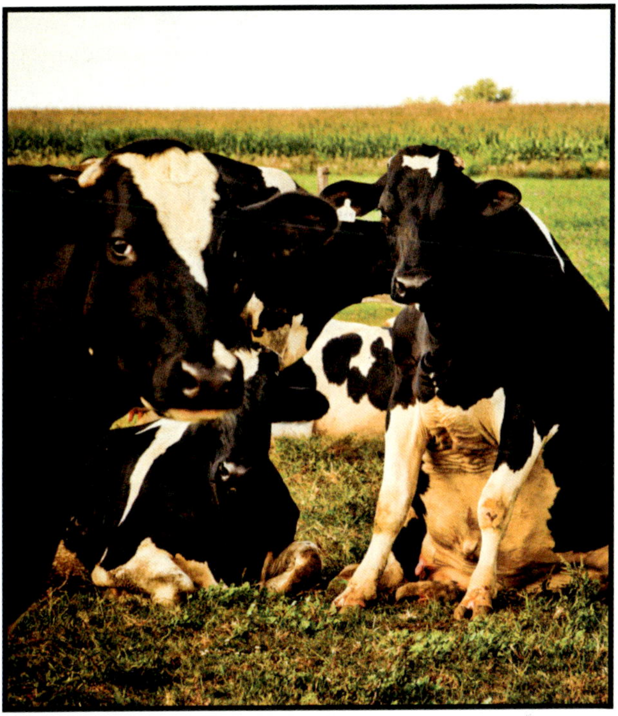

Sitting Milk Cow

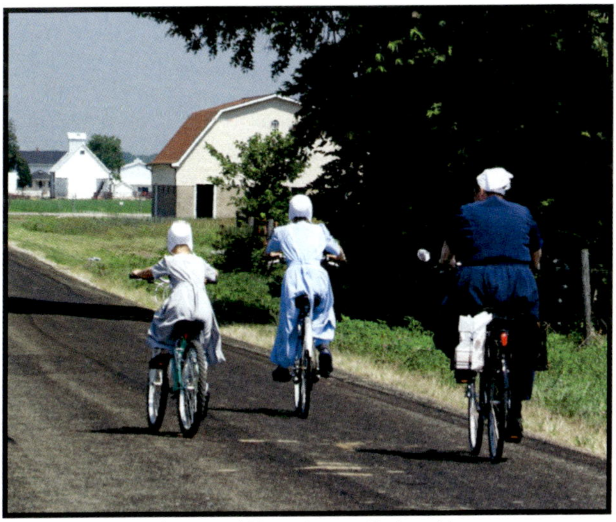

Mother and Daughters Going Home

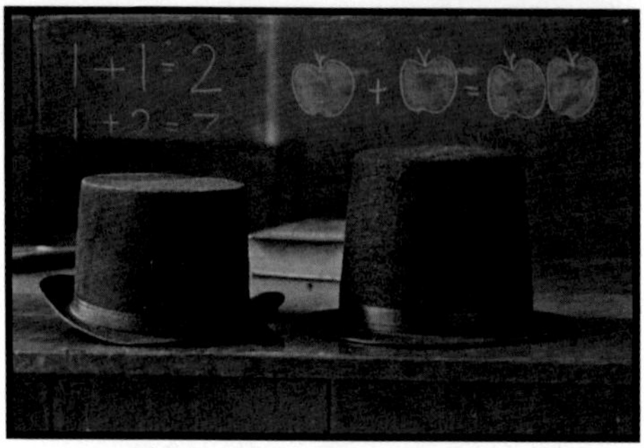

Old School house in Village

and homemade rolls and cookies ...

Rockome Gardens

This beautiful, unusual 200 acre area has a long history of owners and changes but it is a "must see" because you can experience so many things **Amish** in one place. Here are a few things you can expect to see: **horse and buggy ride, rock walls and gardens, Amish museum, Amish home, log structure, benches, farm equipment, barn with buggies, school house, blacksmith barn, windmill, thousands of rock structures, flowers, and horse barn.** Whew! In other words photo op heaven.

The Rockome Restaurant is hog heaven and another must. You can add five pounds just smelling the wonderful things cooking. NOTE: The Rockome Gardens and Restaurant are closed through the winter and reopen in May. For more information www.rockome.com.

Approximate mileage from Downtown St. Louis: 150 miles.

Directions: From St. Louis it is about a 2.5 hour drive. Take I-70 East to Effingham. In Effingham you will take I-57 North to Exit 203 at Arcola. Proceed West (left) on Route 133 into Arthur.

Handicap Accessibility: Excellent since most everything can be viewed from the car. However, you do need to walk through the Rockome Gardens. The paths are flat and paved.

Food: Good grief, are you kidding me!

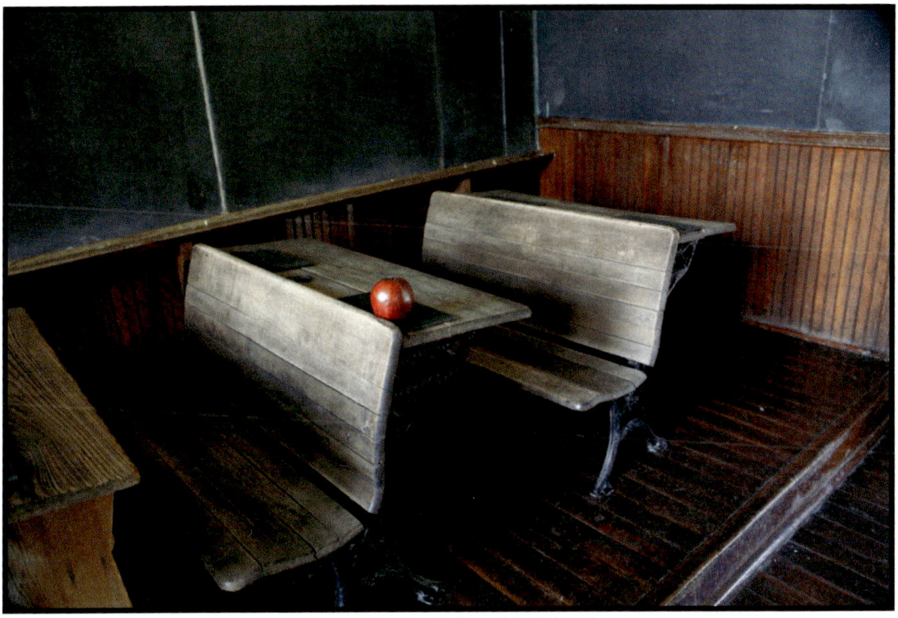

Desks in the Old Amish School

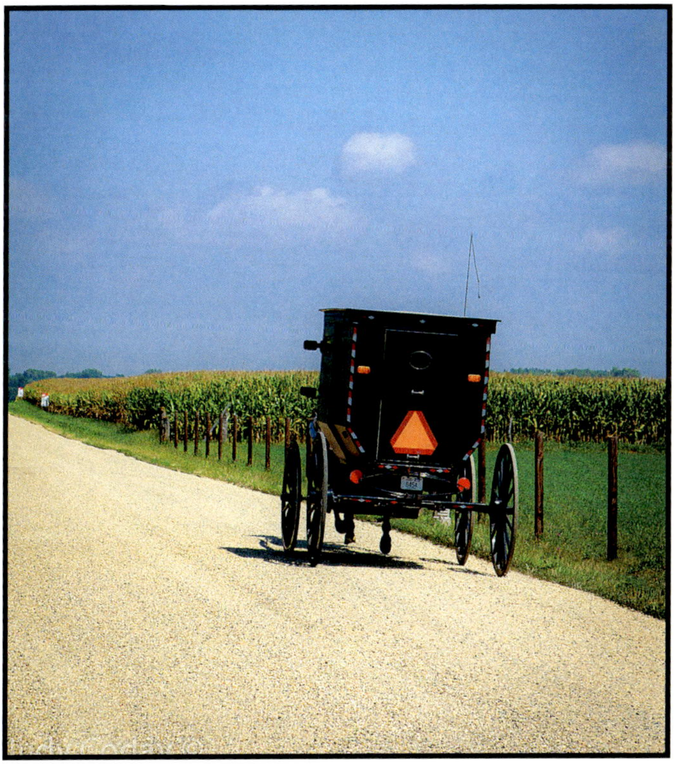

Horse and Buggy Headed Down Country Road

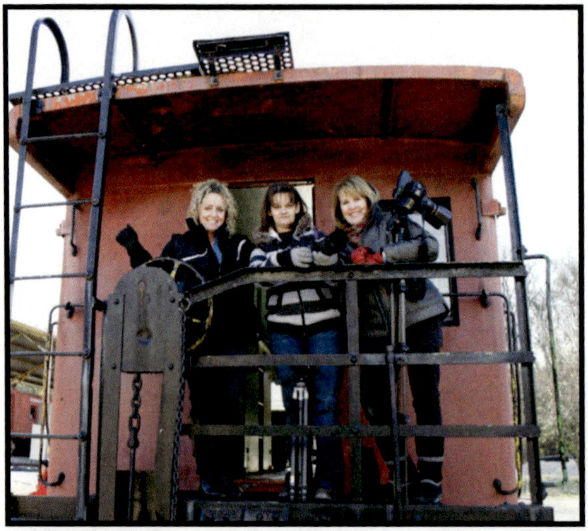

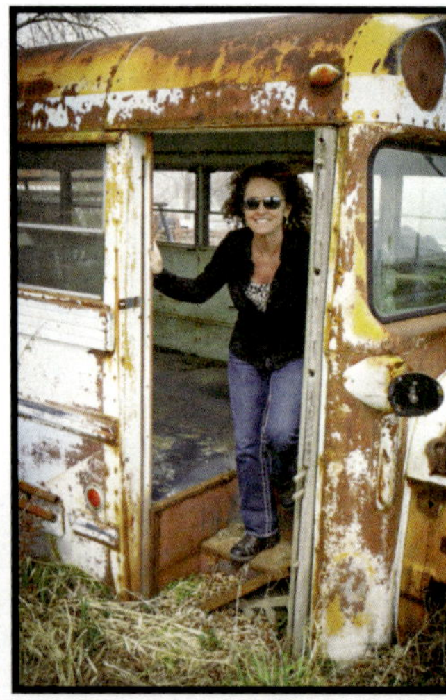

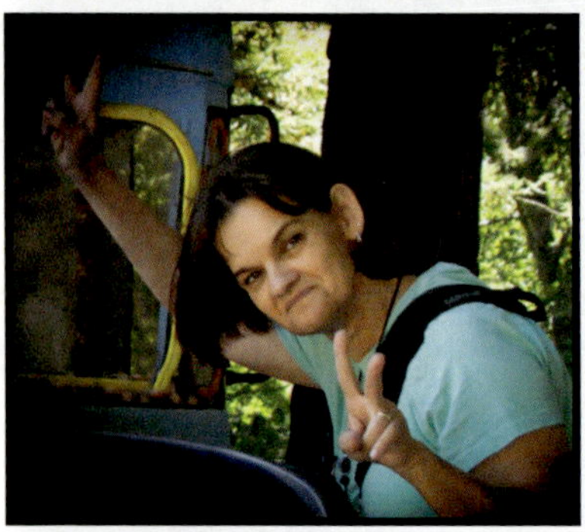

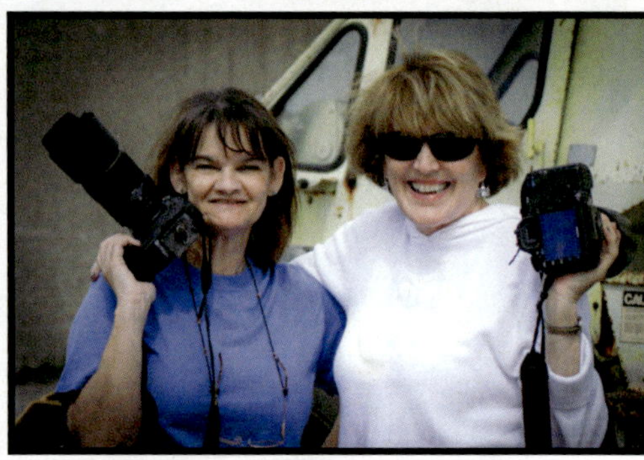

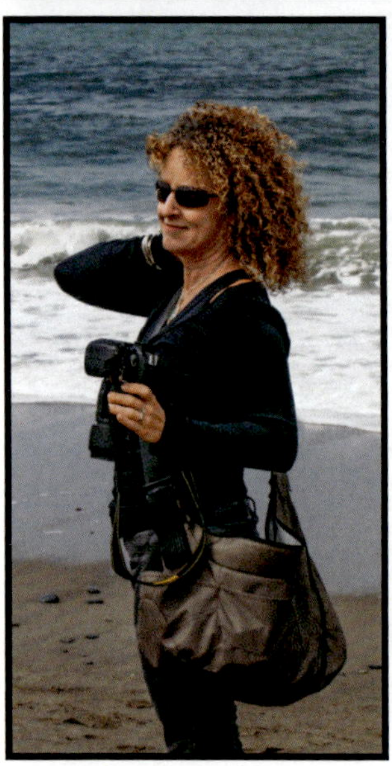

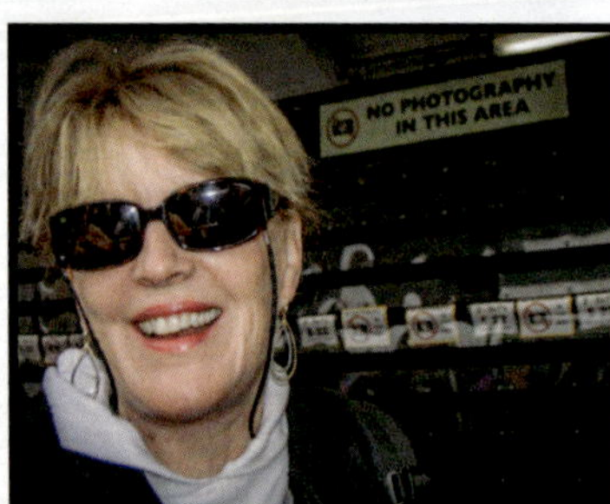
NO PHOTOGRAPHY
IN THIS AREA

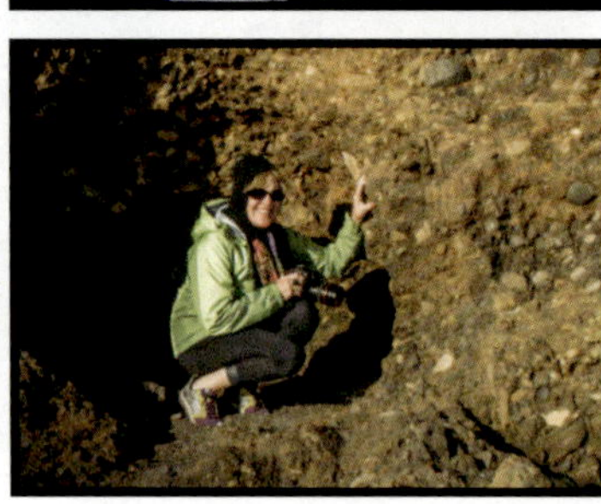

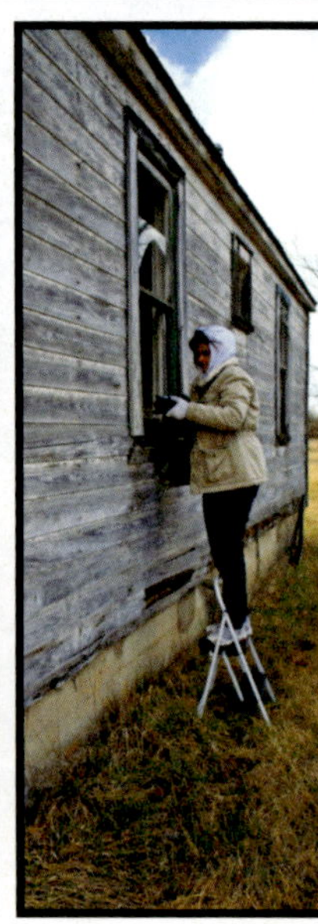

TWENTY~SEVEN

HOW TO BE A MORON WITH OR WITHOUT A CAMERA

The Owl Man

As we all know, you are NOT supposed to go wandering off with strangers; however, this was one of those times that we had the Photographer Stupids. It's very contagious. One person in the herd decides photographing something is a good idea and then like a bunch of sheep, the rest of us follow.

It was a late winter afternoon and a bunch of us were in Forest Park just looking around for something, anything, to shoot. We were getting desperate to hear our cameras whirring and clicking. (We make fun of hunters who will fire at anything that moves. We do try not to actually kill anything with our cameras.)

The place was fairly deserted but off to our left, we saw a rather large man decked out in a camouflage jacket & hood coming toward us. He said, *"Would you all like to see some owls nesting?" "Of course,"* we echoed, nodding our heads. At last! Something to shoot! He began heading towards the woods, and we did what we all have lectured our children about NOT doing, only a million times … we followed. As we approached the path into the woods, it suddenly dawned on us that we didn't KNOW this person and here we were, obediently following him to God knows where.

Have you ever been scared and suddenly break out into uncontrollable giggling at your stupidity? Here were a bunch of grown women willingly following this stranger into the woods. The giggling quickly became guffawing at our stupidity, stumbling over ourselves with laughter imagining our stranger saying things like, *"Here little girl, want a puppy or some candy." "Want to see my camera?"*

As we became totally out of control one of us decided to ask him who he was (like that would make a difference when they found our bodies the next day). He answered, *"I'm known as the Owl Man."* Well, that sent us into more eyebrow raising and snickering behind hands, imagining the headlines the next day, "Owl Man Murders Giggling Women." Not seeing the humor, the Owl Man told us to quit making so much noise as we were scaring the owls. He pointed up in a tree and sure enough, there were owls nesting. Thank God – we were safe! We knew he had a camera when he approached us earlier, but hey, that could have just been a guise to get us to follow. It worked. Later we learned that there really is an Owl Man and he's been studying various owls in Forest Park for years. We still felt really stupid for following him into the woods, camera or not.

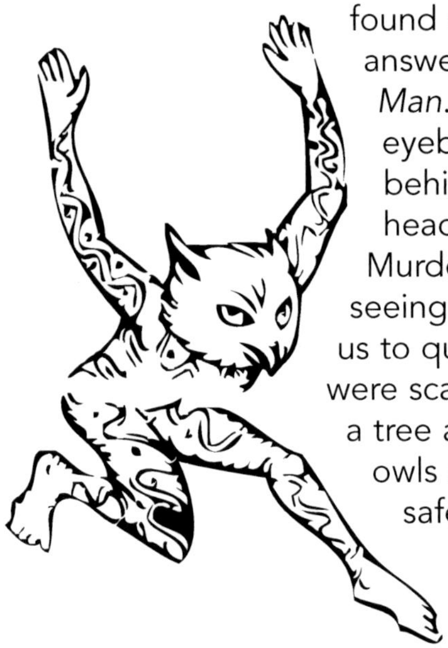

Continental Breakfast Anyone?

These Road Warrior trips usually cause us to work up an appetite. Actually, anything works up our appetite.

During a trip to Amish Country in Indiana, we decided to stay overnight at some hotel along the interstate. Having high standards, we cautiously pulled into the parking lot to check out the place. Clean sheets and hot water are high on the criteria list and we are very clear about that. Upon entering the lobby we noticed a sign that said "Free Continental Breakfast." To hell with our criteria list. FREE FOOD! We registered.

The next morning, one of us beat the other one down to the breakfast bar (I won't say which one) and as I approached I noticed Nancy fussing at the waffle machine. "*What's the matter?*" I asked. She replied, "*This damn machine won't make waffles. Look, it keeps running all over the place!*"

Being the culinary expert on fine French dining, like Chateau Blanc and Jacque en zee Box, I said, "*Here, let me try. It doesn't look like you have enough batter.*" and I applied another scoopful. While this overloaded waffle was cooking (and smoking I might add), I began looking around trying to decide how many buffet items I could get on one very small plate. Spying the milk gravy (love that over biscuits) I began scooping (o.k., shoveling) the gravy on my biscuits, but I did notice it was really thick. Ugh. I hate thick gravy.

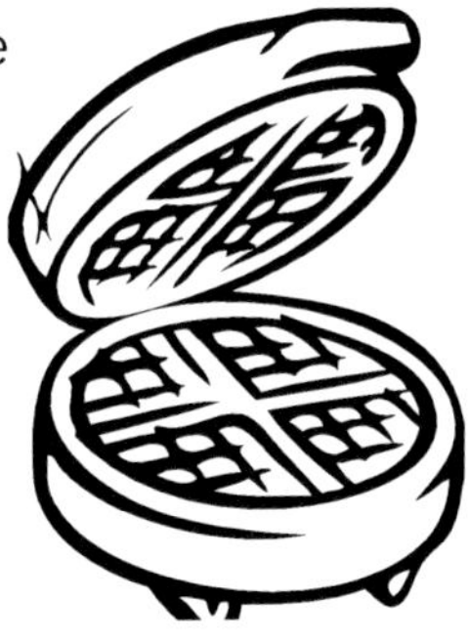

Nancy was still fussing at the "*^&^$#" waffle maker when it suddenly dawned on me. I was shoveling waffle batter onto my biscuits and we had been literally pouring the milk gravy into the waffle maker. When I told Nancy what we had done, we burst into a fit of giggles, which sent the manager scurrying over to see what was going on. By this time the waffle maker was really smoking and the manager, muttering under his breath, waving off the smoke and shaking his head, asked "*What is going on? What is going on?*" Gee, asking us just one time would have been enough.

Nancy, being quick on her feet, replied, "*Oh I don't think we are very hungry after all and we are late for an appointment.*" What appointment? We were 150 miles from home. Sometimes it's just better to cut your losses and get out of town.

How to Throw Your Friend Under the Bus; or What B.N. Did For Love

Bad Nancy and I took a week-long road trip to several fabulous places and ... we fell in love. No, not B.N. and I, but with one of the park rangers at a location we will blog about later. Honestly, he looked like a combination of Brad Pitt and Robert Redford. When he spoke to us on the morning of our unintentional five-mile hike his exact words to us were, "*Have a good walk and good luck.*" Those few words cinched it for us. This was definitely love. Being totally infatuated with this gorgeous man, we failed to pick up on his "good luck" statement.

The previous day when we arrived at this Best-Road-Trip-Ever place it was almost dusk and was ready to close. We briefly gathered some information from another great park ranger and decided we would walk to a **waterfall** the next morning because the ranger said it was only two and a half miles. HAH! We could walk two and a half miles; obviously not thinking clearly that we had to walk two and a half miles back! What idiots.

On the morning of our "walk" we loaded up our gear – tripods, cameras, lens, water and snacks and headed off. This was one of those "walks" where every turn caused one of those "OOOOHH – WOW – AHHHH" reactions. Just unbelievable beauty and photo ops "out the wazoo."

As we reached our final destination (one of the many gorgeous waterfalls) it started to rain. No, not just rain, but POUR. Never fear, being the prepared hikers that we aren't, we started covering our gear with plastic food bags. To hell with us. We weren't going to melt. We wanted to keep shooting. We stayed and took more pictures until it dawned on one of us, "OMG – we have to walk all the way BACK. Who's bright idea was this??"

We sucked it up – like we had other choices since no one was in sight. The first quarter mile we only stopped twice to rest. The next quarter mile became shear agony. B.N. has knee problems and among other things, I have back problems. Everything was starting to throb and hurt. "*Let's try calling the ranger station and see if someone can come out and get us.*" I begged. "*Tell them I passed out on the trail or something.*" Nancy, being the stubborn person she is, muttered, "*Let's frigging keep going!*"

As we struggled on, I remembered that I had lost an eye piece off my camera and thought the last time I had seen it was at cabin about a half mile from our car. Oh God, would we ever see our car again? When we reached the spot where I thought I lost my eye piece, Nancy collapsed on a big rock, while I slugged my way back behind the cabin to search. I searched (more walking) and searched, but no luck. Giving up, I decided to head back to the rock where Nancy was resting.

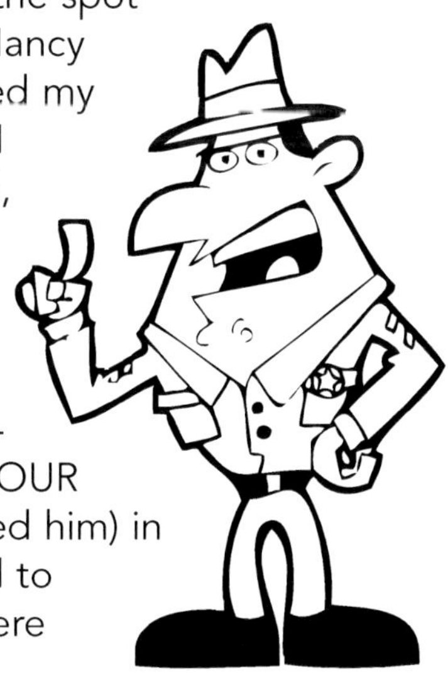

As I came out from behind the cabin – there – hallelujah – was the LOVE OF OUR LIFE – Dandy Randy (yup we nicknamed him) in his golf cart. Oh My God - - - I wanted to bawl my eyes out in pure relief. We were being rescued!! With a surge of adrenaline, and forgetting about my aches and pains, I began running toward them waving my arms, "HAL-LAY-LOO-YA.....YOU ARE SAVING US!!! (I had totally forgotten to be way cool) I threw myself (no, not into his arms – wanted to, but B.N. was already there. No, not really) along with my gear into his golf cart. Nancy was already seated and I noticed she had a huge smile wrapped around her face (you know, the cat who ate the canary kind). Dandy Randy said he figured we'd had enough. What?? He didn't think we looked like outdoor pioneer women in our designer jackets and tennis shoes with wet and frizzy hair? At least we had changed from our sandals into sturdier shoes. Well, you can't look good all the time.

The last half mile "home" was bliss as we tried to contain our drooling and adoringly held on to Dandy's every word as he drove us back. Too quickly we arrived at the car and as he pulled off and waved, we blabbered our thank-you's once again.

Plopping our tired butts into the car, I noticed that Bad Nancy had this confessional look on her face. "*What?*" I said. "*You look guilty.*"

"*Well,*" she huffed, "*I can't believe you came running up to the golf cart back there. You were supposed to be in pain! You were supposed to be hobbling like you had been doing the last 2 miles.*"

Here came BN's confession: "*When Randy stopped I jumped up off the rock so he wouldn't see me sprawled out and panting for breath. He asked if we'd had enough walking.*"
"*I told him **I** was fine but my friend (i.e. ME) was really hurting and she could sure use a ride back. I didn't want him to think I was a weakling. Then, there you came … running!!*"
Some days you have to throw your friend under the bus, in the name of love.

TWENTY~EIGHT

WHAT TO DO WITH ALL THOSE PHOTOGRAPHS!

A Serious Moment

The "digital revolution" has taken something from us. While it's true that it's now so affordable and easy to snap away with our various cameras, cell phones, iPads and what-have-yous, are we stripping photography of its amazing powers to keep the past in our sights?

This is why we are including this chapter in our book. We know there are so many of you out there that easily take thousands of pictures and then casually, delete from iPhones and other digital gadgets. It's not like any of us have a ton of free time to make albums like we did "in the old days." But, before you snap and casually delete, consider these thoughts.

Never will your past become so significant as when you lose a loved one.

When my own mother and father passed away, over 10 years ago, I dreaded going through all their personal possessions, especially the boxes of photographs I drug home with me. I was overwhelmed. Finally, the day came when I knew I had to tackle that job. As I plowed through boxes, I found myself back in the past, not sobbing in grief, but finding a strange kind of peace and understanding of our lives.

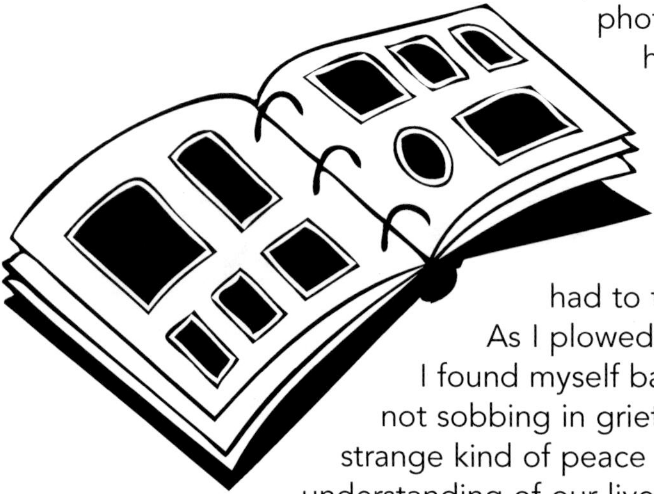

As part of my grieving process, I remember taking some of my favorite photographs, framing them and placing them on a wooden tray, which I placed on a library table in our living room. Every time I passed this tray, some magical healing took place. It is with peace and loving that I now, easily, gaze at those photographs and remember all the good times we had as a family. I even made an album (the real kind you hold in your hand) for my brother and discovered the pasting and gluing to be another healing step in my grieving process. I remember the day I gave it to him and big tears rolled down his cheeks. This from the tough-guy "kid brother" who was always playing with army men and wrapping old blankets around his shoulders so he could jump off our porch to fly like Superman.

My grown children still pull out old photographs I have taken of them since birth and look through the various albums and boxes. Another photo keeper, my favorite Aunt Georgie, was a master organizer of photographs and saver of all things. Although she has passed, I will tell you for certain that I cherished, even as a child, going to her house and dragging out all her photo albums, spending countless hours thumbing through our family history.

Never Underestimate the Power of Your Photographs

So for whatever reason you may have for snapping away, get those photographs out of your digital devices and take a look at all the fabulous ideas for displaying your creations. Obviously, these are not all our ideas (I've heard that there really isn't anything that's an "original idea" but that's for another time).

IDEAS

Old frames, in any shape, as long as they hold together, add character and texture to images. This is an old window frame we found in a pile of junk at a tear-down site. We left the paint, peeling and all, and sprayed it with a liquid varnish to hold the pieces in tact. Next, we added chicken wire (yup you really can buy this stuff at the hardware store and it's not just for chickens) which we stapled on the back. The little clothes pins were bought at an art store in The Loop, but you can buy regular clothes pins at any store (maybe not Nordstrom's or Saks). This creates an instant

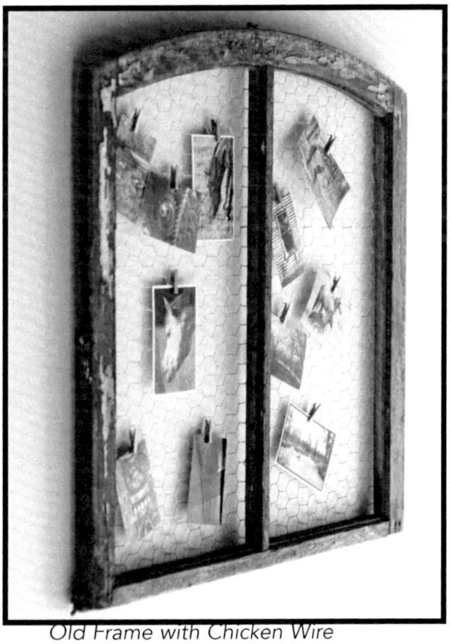

Old Frame with Chicken Wire

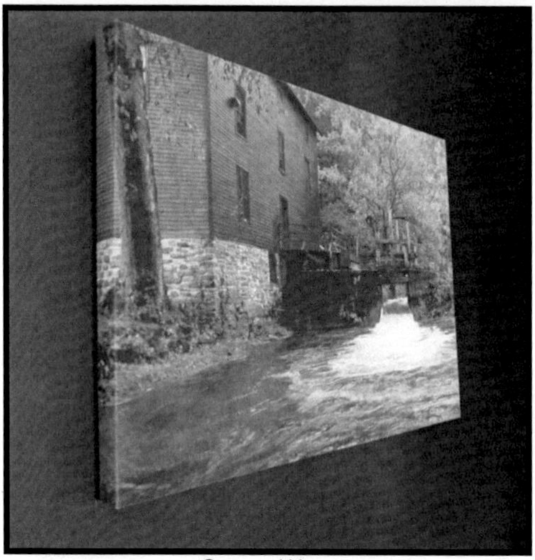

Canvas Wrap

display and it's easy to change out your photographs.

Canvas wrapped photographs have become very popular and available at all photo developing stores

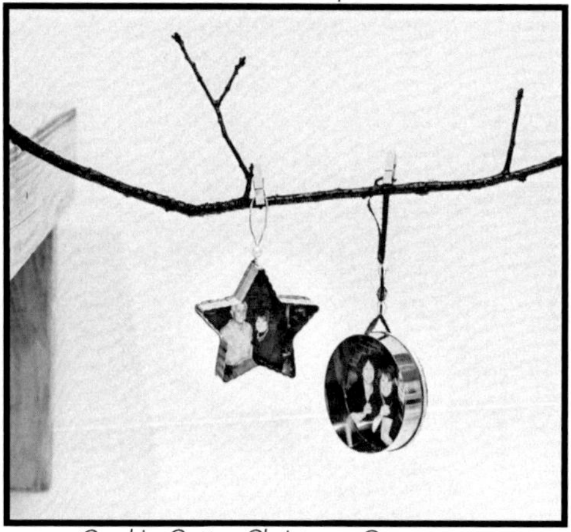

Cookie Cutter Christmas Ornaments

A Non-Fattening Use for Cookie Cutters

This idea is from a very clever friend, Angie Meyers, and she gave these to me as a Christmas present one year. Who would have thought of using cookie cutters (the tin ones without backs). She took these photos at a dinner party at my house, then had them printed. Tracing the shape of the cookie cutter, she made a back out of heavy cardboard, which she covered with colored paper. She added the colored ribbon with a bead and I have a forever gift, which I put on our tree every year. Thank you, again, Angie!

To Heck With Hanging Up Clothes!

Nancy uses this idea in her laundry room and we thought it turned out neat-o.

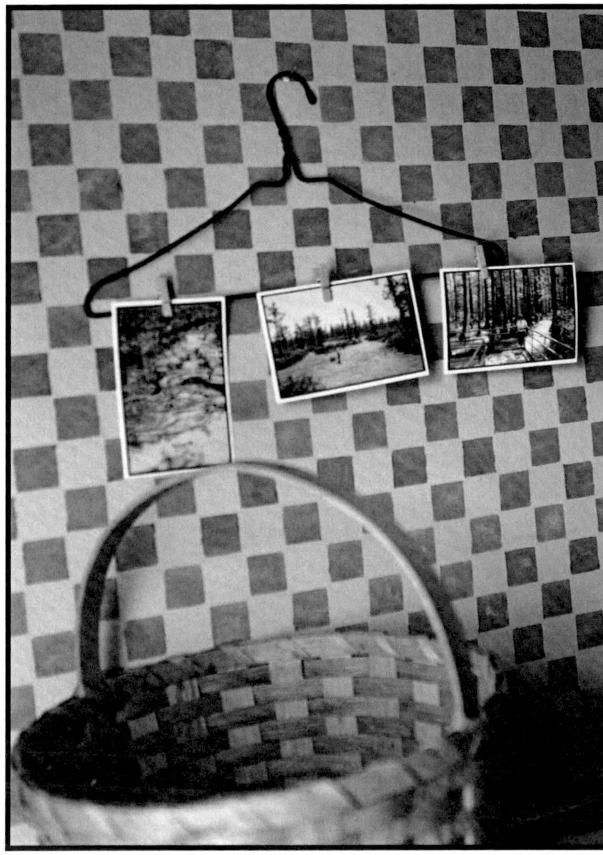

Coat Hanger with Photos

Have a corner in your child's bedroom that needs "something"? Here I used a piece of cloth clothesline and regular clothes pins. I attached the rope to either corner. Presto.

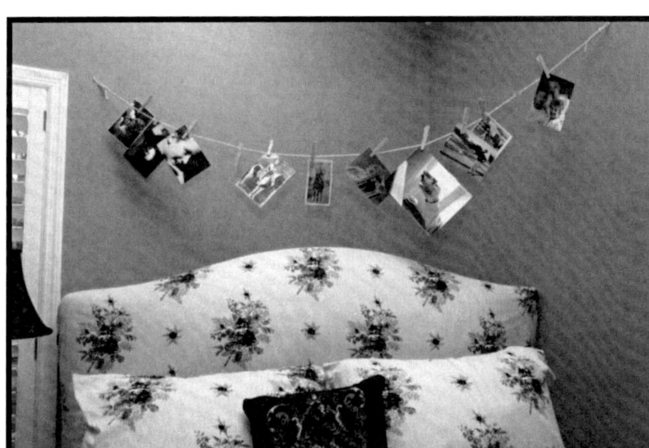

Clothesline with Pictures Hung by Clothes Pins

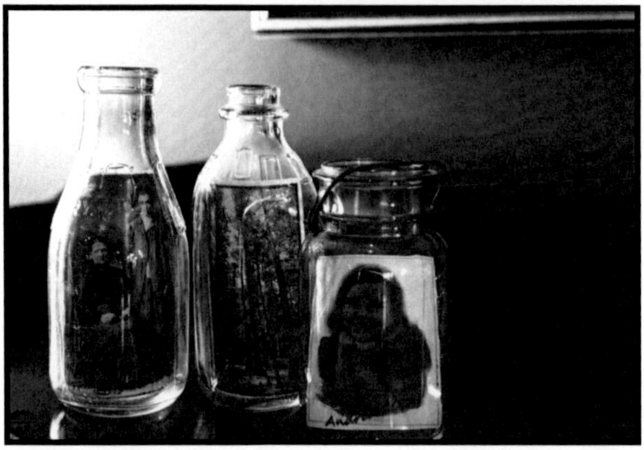

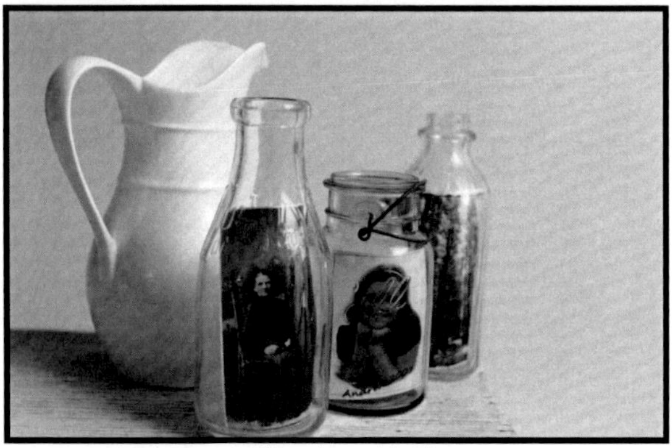

Glass Jars with Photos

GLASS JARS HAVE MORE USES. This should be a headline. Clear glass works best. Here we used a mason jar, along with a couple of old bottles and just rolled the photograph, gently so it doesn't crease. Then drop it down into the jar. When you release it unfolds itself into the jar space.

Since we photograph weddings from time to time we always photograph the table centerpieces. One bride had placed sand from the beach where they were married (and maybe out of their swimming suits) and a burning candle into regular glass jars.

Hopefully, she lit the candle after the candle was placed in the sand. I learned this the hard way after setting several paper bags, with sand in them to use as luminaries, on fire. Boy they go up in flames fast.

Pulling from her idea we thought it would be great to have the bride and groom's engagement picture inside, on each table, and perhaps a flower or two or pebbles or who knows what. Then, these could be favors if guests wanted to take them home.

A FEW MORE GEMS

Cable Photo Holder

This little gem has a variety of uses besides holding photographs. It is a wire covered with green plastic (they come in black, white, red, blue and green) with a loop at one end to hang from the ceiling and a weight on the other so it hangs straight. It comes with little magnets and you place a photograph or card or whatever on the string and attach with one of the little magnets.

The wire is magnetic, too, so your photos hang in a line, or however you decide to hang it. See their website: www.kikkerland.com. We got ours at Blick Art Materials in The Loop (Delmar) in St. Louis, University City.

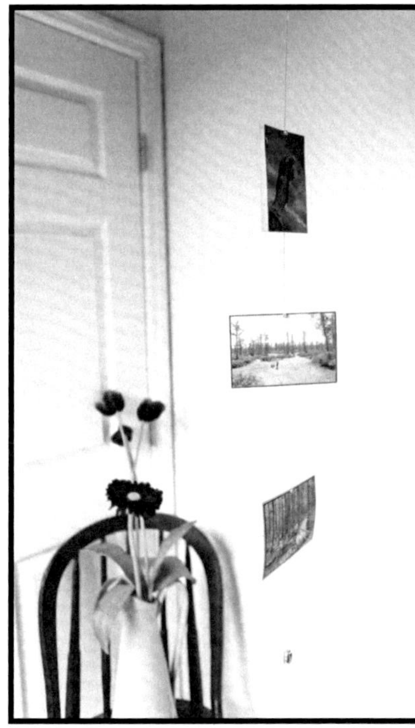

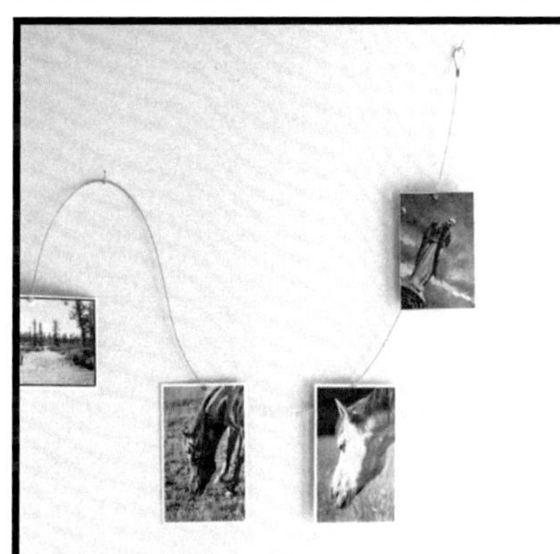

Hanging Cable Photo Holder

Love Isn't Love Until You Give It Away

Cards

A very clever guy and his doubly clever wife, gave me this idea. They buy inexpensive, blank notecards and make 3 x 5 photo prints, which they keep in a shoebox. When they need to send a note or greeting card, they pull out an appropriate photo, glue it to the front of the notecard, and the recipients get a Jeff or Donna original. Call me old-fashioned, but there's something so civilized about a handwritten note, as opposed to emails. Receiving a note you can hold in your hand, just seems so much more thoughtful. Thank you, Jeff Hirsch and Donna Parrone!

I have purchased 40 blank notecards, on sale, at Michaels, including envelopes, for around $5 a box. I also use either glue sticks or Elmer's Craft Bond, acid Free/Photo Safe Rubber Cement to attach the photographs.

For a little more money and a very professional look for individual photographs (about $1.20 a card and you don't have to buy huge quantities) I use a company called The Photographer's Edge. Go online to get your free catalog at **www.photographersedge.com**. They also come with envelopes.

Little Bitty Individual Photo Albums

Ugh. Who wants to go to all that trouble. These little albums are about as easy as it gets and make such great gifts. Again, you can glue your photographs right onto the page. Go to **www.kolo-usa.com.** They come in various colors and tie closed with a coordinating ribbon. I have purchased them locally at art stores and Creve Coeur Camera. The price runs between $6 and $10.

Hardback Books

Yes we said books – real books like with hard covers – you can hold in your hand, with bound pages. Talk about the ultimate gift! I do not consider myself a technical genius by any stretch of the imagination but even I have been able to download software and have made many books over the years for wedding presents, birthday gifts, thank-you's for a vacation,

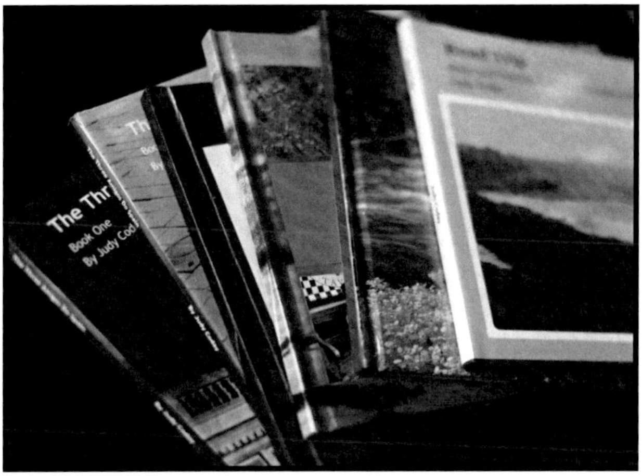

Hard Back Photo Books

Christmas presents – and I love going back and re-enjoying an event through my photographs.

You don't need a high-powered camera to do these books because they have templates and warnings if your image will turn out blurry. Even if your image shows up blurry, just make it smaller using their handy "sizers." I have even used older images I have scanned and they worked out just fine. Yup, even cell phone photographs work.

These books vary greatly in price and the companies I recommend not only offer great quality and good pricing, but ease for the "not so technical wizards." If you are seriously a geek and a creative genius with money to burn there are dozens of choices out there.

My favorite is Mixbook. I have found their quality superb and they offer a huge variety of backdrops, styles, color, font, ease, etc. Or, if you don't want to use their templates, you can drag your pictures over to blank pages and place them anywhere you want on the page. You can also place your text anywhere you want on these blank pages. Then, you can add background, color, whatever, and change as you need.

AND THEN, THERE'S "REGULAR" FRAMING

Bad Nancy is our bargain hunter extraordinaire and she's done it again. She decided to have one of her prints framed. Of course you can always frame things yourself, which we have all done, but invariably as soon as you get the print into the frame and flip it back over, some mysterious piece of dog hair or lint ends up stuck under the glass and then you have to take the whole thing apart because you know that little piece of whatever is going to stand out like a pimple on prom night.

She headed to Hobby Lobby, armed with a 40% off coupon that she got online and her 16 x 12 color print that she wanted framed. Printing color photographs that size runs about $10. As you may or may not know, Hobby Lobby has a great framing department. They cut a custom matt for $7 (used her 40% off coupon here); she bought a frame in the store with glass and then sweet-talked the person in the frame department to put the matte and the picture into the frame for her. The frame size ended up being 23 x 19 for which she paid $15 and she ended up with a beautifully framed, great piece of artwork for about $30! Now that is more than reasonable.

Make Your Own Book Websites:

www.mixbook.com
www.blurb.com
www.shutterfly.com
www.flikr.com

Other Goodie Ideas

Here are a few other ideas that might interest you:

- Who doesn't need "vintage charm"? Use a meaningful family photo to add something special to gifts. **Photocopy an older black-and-white image** (honor copyrights!) and stick this photo to plain butcher paper (I buy this by the roll at Michaels) and add a red ribbon.

- If you really want your loved ones close to you, have a photo made into a shower curtain. www.photoshowercurtain.com

- Don't like to sleep alone? Make your photographs into pillowcases. www.snapfish.com

- Here is another fun way to label bottles of wine or jars of cookie mix or whatever concoction you like to make. www.pinholepro.com

- Pick your favorite photo and order a smartphone cover called Simply Cellies. www.simplycolorlab.com

- Ah, the good old days. Remember **Photo Booths** and the little strip of 3 or 4 pictures that would develop right there for you? Now you can have your photographs made into **Photo Booth filmstrips** like we used to get for 50 cents and a smile. www.prodpi.com

- Kids' photographs make such good **Christmas ornaments** and great grandparent gifts. www.blackriverimaging.com

- Have your photograph made into **photo stickers** to use as address labels for Christmas Cards or gift tags www.whcc.com

- Here's an easy way to frame your photographs. **Frameless wall decor** is easy to use and will add a splash of color and style to a space. You don't need a hammer or nail to hang the mat. Each matte comes with a display kit containing adhesive foam mounting squares. The squares stick to the back of the matte and then the wall. The matte is the decorative frame. Each matte features trendy patterns. www.windiemats.com

- Make your own **refrigerator magnets** out of your photographs by using adhesive magnet paper (it comes in a 12" x 24" sheet.) You peel away the magnet's adhesive side and place your photos atop the adhesive. Smooth out any bubbles before cutting out your images. www.promagproducts.com

TWENTY~NINE

GENERAL TIPS FOR THE ASPIRING PHOTOGRAPHER

"General Tips That Every Photographer Has Learned the Hard Way and It Cost a Bundle of Money to Fix or Unnecessary Agony and Hair Pulling."

- The only way to learn is to shoot more and the way to make yourself shoot more is to give yourself an assignment, and make each assignment last a week. As time goes by, make the assignments harder and last more than a week. Here are a few examples of assignments: hands, flowers, old doors, close-ups, energy, outside looking in or inside looking out, broken windows, hats, bird's eye view, etc.

- When you are done for the day, be sure to change your camera settings back to the ones you use most often.

- Make sure your battery is fully charged before hitting the road.

- Put a LED flashlight in your camera bag. A flashlight can be used for many things, even for extra light when shooting in the dark.

- Always format your memory card – in your camera – and not on the computer. Formatting a memory card wipes the card completely clean and it is ready to go the next time.

- Delete bad shots (out of focus, bad lighting, etc) in your camera as you go. You will get more shots per card this way.

- Protect the lens glass on your camera with a UV filter. If you scratch the UV filter that's very sad, but that is better than scratching an expensive lens.

- Don't change your lens in dusty weather. Hold your camera down toward the ground and opposite from the wind. If at all possible, get in your car or indoors.

- If shooting in cold weather, have extra batteries. Cold weather can drain a battery quickly.

- Research ahead of time, places you are going to photograph. Most phones now have an app that will show you times for sunrise and sunset.

- To save brainpower, photograph the signs of places you are shooting so when you get home and start going through all your photographs you won't have to say, "Where in the hell did I take this one?"

When we first started with this out-of-control hobby if a view didn't present itself as immediately scenic or an incredible vista, we kept wandering around trying to find something to shoot.

- If you see something that makes you stop, find out why. Don't just look, shoot and leave. Learn to see the world around you and get creative. Use different exposures, angles, get down on your stomach (yes, I have had someone come along while in this position to ask me if I was alright). Look for color, patterns, texture and leading lines. Make a checklist to take with you the next time.

- Learn the rule of thirds. The Rule of Thirds is a guideline for creating an interesting composition by not necessarily placing your subject square in the middle of the photograph. The guideline proposes that an image should be imagined as divided into nine equal parts by two equally-spaced horizontal lines and two equally-spaced vertical lines, and that important compositional elements should be placed along these lines or their intersections. Proponents of the technique claim that aligning a subject with these points creates more tension, energy and interest in the composition than simply centering the subject.

- When photographing people try to make sure there is a catch light in their eyes. This is the little, tiny, light that reflects in the pupils and gives the eyes sparkle and interest. It is most often caused by a camera flash, but can be created by using a reflector to bounce light into the eyes.

- Before snapping your picture, run your eye around the viewfinder and check for unwanted objects, like trees, telephone lines, road signs and things coming out of your subject's head.

- Learn to use a tripod. It's a good habit to get into because of "camera shake" which is really you breathing (sometimes necessary) or hands slightly moving, causing blur. Tripods are necessary for low light or evening shooting because you are using slow shutter speeds. The self-timer on the camera is a good thing to use, too.

- When you think you are close to your subject, take the shot and then move in closer. Fill the frame with your subject.

- Do you want to show size? Place a person in the shot next to trees, buildings or even smaller things and this will show proportion and help the viewer see just how big or small your subject is. See page 118 for an example

- If you have to shoot through a window, here are a couple of tips. Turn off all the lights in the room. This will stop reflection in the glass. If outdoors, shooting in through a window, try using your hand over the lens to stop reflection. You can also try putting your camera lens right on the window.

Exposure Tips

- If you are not sure what exposure to use, use your camera's auto bracketing. (Not all cameras have this, but if you do, be sure to learn how to use it.)

- The smallest aperture number gives the widest opening – more light and more depth of field.

- The largest aperture number gives less light and means more sharpness or detail.

- When depth of field is not a concern, use f/8 or f/11 as either one of these will offer the greatest sharpness throughout the scene.

- If your camera has Aperture Priority, start with it and the camera will pick the correct shutter speed. For example: On a clear or sunny day, use f/16; on a hazy or light contrast, use f/8; on an overcast or heavy heavy overcast day, use f/5.6.

- If exposure baffles you (and believe me it has us all baffled at times), remember the Sunny 16 Rule but you have to know how to read ISO or "film speed" (we told you we were seniors and not the high school kind).

- The sunny f/16 rule, or Basic Daylight Exposure (BDE for short), tells you that the proper exposure in digital photography for a front lit subject is f/16 with a shutter speed of 1/ISO (that's 1 over the ISO in use). According to the sunny f/16 rule, at ISO 100, BDE would be f/16 at 1/100 second, and at ISO 200, BDE would be f/16 at 1/200 second. When taking photos on a bright, sunny day, set the ISO of your camera to 100, the aperture to f/16, and the shutter to 1/100 second. Then go out and take pictures of some front lit subjects. As long as your subject isn't white or black, the exposures should be great. No metering necessary.

Here are some of our favorite books and all are available on Amazon (www.amazon.com). We usually buy the "used" ones because they are half the price and in very good condition.

Books to Read

Exposure Photo Workshop *by Jeff Wignall*
The Complete Guide to Night and Low-Light Photography *by Lee Frost*
Understanding Exposure, Revised Edition *by Bryan Peterson*
The Digital Photographer's Guide to Exposure *by Peter Cope*
Learning to See Creatively, Revised Edition *by Bryan Peterson*
Creative Nature & Outdoor Photography *by Brenda Tharp*
Practical HDR Second Edition *by David Nightingale*
The HDR Book *by Rafael* *"RC" Concepcion*
The Moment it Clicks *by Joe McNally*

Our Favorite Editing Software

Elements 10	www.adobe.com
CS (Photoshop)	www.adobe.com
Lightroom (LR4)	www.adobe.com
Nik Software	www.niksoftware.com
Photomatix	www.hdrsoft.com
Topaz Image Enhancing	www.topaz.com
Portrait Professional	www.portraitprofessional.com
Alien Skin	www.alienskin.com

Our Favorite Magazines

American Photo
Popular Photography
Shutterbug
Outdoor Photographer
Professional Photographer
Click

Fun Websites to Teach You Online

Kelbytraining.com	$24.95/month
Lynda.com	$25/month *(subscribe or unsubscribe monthly)*
Youtube.com	Free and has tons of learning videos
DIY.com	Free and several photography workshops

Classes and Workshops Available in the St. Louis Area

STLPA (St. Louis Photo Authority)
Project Space at 858 Hodiamont Avenue,
Saint Louis, Missouri, 63112
Classes, Meet Ups, Studio Rental
Edward Crim 314-504-6692
http://www.edwardcrim.com

Jeff Hirsch Digital Imaging Services
Certified Expert Lightroom Photoshop
Private and Individual Classes
(314) 249-5100
jeff@jeffhirsch.com
http://www.jeffhirsch.com

Photo-Resource-Center of St. Louis
Kathy O'Donnell 314-323-4400
odonnellkm@sbcglobal.net
photo-resourse-center.com
Photography Instruction All Levels

St. Louis Photoshop Meetup
Studio 314 – Steve Grappe & Jasen Vinlove
314-720-1707
www.meetup.com/photoshop-250/

Photography Clubs
Missouri

www.saintlouisphotogaphyclub.com
www.meetup.com
www.photoclubstl.com
www.stlcameraclub.com

THIRTY

TIPS AND FAVORITE PLACES TO SHOOT FROM THE ST. LOUIS PRO'S

These people are the nicest individuals you will ever want to meet and work with, and, we wouldn't put them in here if we didn't think their work was TOPNOTCH!

Nancy Williams 314-420-2589
Nancy Williams Photography

View her work at:	www.idoweddingphotography.net Shares site with partner, Pamela Schneipp Photography Facebook at "I Do Wedding Photography" St. Louis Facebook at "Nancy Williams Photography" St. Louis
Favorite Place to Shoot:	South St. Louis City commercial area near the flood wall Bee Tree Park in South County St. Louis Zoo

Tip for Beginners: Get off auto mode and choose your focus point.

Carla Scuzzo
Carlagraphs
1-303-522-4251 (St. Louis)

View her work at: www.carlagraphs.smugmug.com

Favorite Place to Shoot: Downtown St. Louis. Park and walk. There are amazing buildings with loads of history from the Soulard Market down to the Riverfront (Eads Bridge, Graffiti Wall, the Landing) to the crumbling remains of buildings that have seen better days – you can't go wrong just hoofing it anywhere in the city. St. Louis City is filled with charm, character, gorgeous renovations and sweet dilapidation.

Favorite Tip: In portraiture, emotion is key. A photographer can have a beautiful background, stellar lighting, and the best camera in the whole wide world, but if none of the essence of the subject is captured, the image will die and all those good elements will be for naught. Take the time to loosen up your subjects – it will be well worth it.

Kymberlie Birkenkamp 314-616-5080
Misfit Hue Photography

View her work at:	kymberlieblu@att.net/misfithuephotography on Facebook
Favorite Place to Shoot:	My favorite place to shoot is not one particular place but festivals. Go deep into the hoopla of the people and forget yourself. At festivals, people are less troubled by your camera and it's a fantastic way to hone your skills in capturing moments. If festivals aren't for you, go to the Missouri Botanical Garden in the winter. There is so much to see there, even in winter. People rarely think to go there then and it will force you to shoot. That's the point — take yourself out of your comfort zone and you will grow! I do it every chance that I can and am never disappointed.
Favorite Tip:	Change your height, get low, get high, and shoot at an angle to help you see things from a new perspective. Feel free to zoom in close … no closer … closer! LOL

Pamela Schniepp
Pamela Schniepp Photography Pmac59@aol.com

View her work at: www.idoweddingphotography.net Shares site with partner, Nancy Williams Photography, FB at "I Do Wedding Photography" St. Louis

Favorite Place to Shoot: Old Town St. Charles, MO

Angie Wagner 314-606-8661
Gigi Wagner Photography

Favorite Place to Shoot: Main Street in Old St. Charles, Mo.

Favorite Tips:

1. Always schedule a one-year-old's cake smash session after their actual birthday party. Then, they will know what cake is and know exactly what to do with it!
2. When shooting a group of people, put your focal point on the eye of the person closest to you.
3. I always ask the people I'm shooting to get cheeky with each other. The closer the better ... those are my most favorite shots.
4. Have lots of toys and distractions (rattles and bells) ready when you are shooting little ones.
5. Remind your client to make sure their nails/nail polish looks nice. No chips!

Joseph Vitale
Joseph Vitale Photography
josephvitalephotographyu@gmail.com

Favorite Tip: When shooting high school seniors, make the senior feel like a super model. I always try to make sure they have a makeup artist available and then I give them the royal treatment for 2-3 hours. Keeping mom involved is very helpful as well. Know what you want before the shoot by talking with your client and getting to know their personality.

Kristi Evans Lenz
LenzArt Photography
View her work at: www.kristilenz.com
http://about.me/kristilenz

Favorite Place to Shoot: St. Louis County parks. There are over 50 county parks in St. Louis County, ranging from the tiny to the elaborate. At Lone Elk Park you can see elk, bison and deer; Suson Park has a working farm; Simpson Park has a great fishing lake. This does not even begin to scratch the surface of photography opportunities available at these parks. Check out St. Louis county parks, especially some of the more out of the way ones. You will be pleasantly surprised!

Brooke Boyer
Brooke Boyer Photography brooke.boyer09@gmail.com

View her work at: www.brookeboyerphotography.com
www.blog.brookeboyerphotography.com

Favorite place to shoot: Quail Ridge Park, St. Charles County — gorgeous color in the fall!

Shooting Tip: If shooting in the City, always shoot with a buddy.

Meghan Stewart
The Magpie Project Photography 314-960-4235
meghandstewart@gmail.com

Favorite places to shoot:

1. The Mercy Center on Geyer Road in the fall – great for family shoots
2. Downtown Kirkwood in the late afternoon/early evening, especially the alleys on the north side of Argonne across from the train station
3. Meeting House and old burying ground on Geyer Road in Frontenac
4. The Transportation Museum – 3015 Barrett Station Road – great outdoor location with cool old trains
5. City Garden, downtown St. Louis
6. Near Cadet, Missouri are lots of old barns and pretty rolling hills/farmland, etc.

Shooting Tips:

- Try and be still (I get all jumpy when I'm excited which doesn't help in capturing a sharp image)
- A noise machine with a fart noise is an excellent tool to have when shooting younger kids, especially boys
- Ask kids for their ideas on posing or what they think would look "cool."
- Asking kids not to smile no matter what, usually results in a great natural smile
- White balance

Jeff Hirsch
Jeff Hirsch Digital Imaging Services 314-249-5100
jeff@jeffhirsch.com

View his work at: www.flickr.com/photos/heff/sets or www.jeffhirsch.com

Favorite place to shoot: Soulard Market on a Saturday morning! Best place to people watch.

Shooting Tip: Shoot from the heart. Don't worry too much about if you have enough gear or what other people think. Find your own photographic voice. Find the way that you and only you see the world and express it in your photos. Authenticity is the key to good photography.

(Editor's note): Jeff is way too modest. He is a Photographer and Photo-Educator, conducts lessons for individuals and groups, Calibration, Asset Management and Other Photographic Tech Support Services, as well as a "Certified Expert in Photoshop and Lightroom." And, he will not make you feel like an idiot!

THIRTY~ONE

Where to Go When the Weather Won't Cooperate

"Ya Just Gotta Gimme Sumpin to Shoot"
(I live in Missouri, after all)

Some days you just have to get out of the house and "shoot something." Unfortunately, our weather doesn't always cooperate, with rain, freezing weather or heat. During a cold spell you feel like Ralphie's little brother, Randy, in The Christmas Story – so bundled up, movement is next to impossible and heaven forbid if you need to make a Pit Stop!

We've all had weather concerns at one time or another so here's a list we started. Hey, if you have other ideas, please go to our blog contained in our website at www.snappinsistas.com

Remember, folks from out of town will be (hopefully) reading this, too, so while some of the places may seem perfectly obvious to you, our out-of-town guests could get those urges to "shoot something" and not have a clue where to go.

The Museum of Transportation
3015 Barret Station Road • St. Louis, MO 63122
314-615-8668
Cost to enter $6-8
If you love, love, love **trains** this is your place. While some of the trains are parked outside, quite a few are under roof so you may get wet walking but it's worth it. There are also two "inside buildings." Our favorite is the **car museum** and there are some great guys that work there. If you ask, they will remove the roping around the cars and allow you to get up close and personal. As they say, "You can get within one inch of the car, but don't go any closer!" The place for **planes**, **trains** and **automobiles**.

The City Museum
701 North 15th Street • St. Louis, MO 63103
314-213-2489
Cost to enter $12.00
This place will stretch your imagination like never before! A three-story **warehouse** of some type in it's day, now houses an absolute treasure trove of **tunnels, slides, architecture, old bank vaults, fish tanks, tree houses, skateboard ramps, hanging rope swings, statuary**, etc You have to look twice at something to actually see what it's made of. We've been there numerous times and still haven't covered every nook and cranny. Plus, there is the roof which holds an old **school bus**, hanging off the side, a **Ferris wheel**, a **slide**, etc., and **great views**, especially at night. There are special hours for the roof. Call ahead.

I should also mention there is a ton of **natural light** due to the old **factory windows**. Many photographers take their clients there for portraits. To our knowledge, there isn't an extra charge for this (just the normal entry fee).

Another Bonus at City Museum

City Museum is the home of **Circus** Harmony, which is a non-profit social circus organization that uses circus arts to motivate social change. The group is made up of young people who do trapeze, vaulting, acrobatics, juggling – all-around entertainers. Jessica Hentoff is the Artistic/Executive Director and she and her team also offer classes in a variety of circus arts for people ages 5 and up. Here is her information:
314-436-7676; www.circusharmony.org;
or email circuslady@circusharmony.org.

The troupes put on shows regularly at City Museum and at various venues around town and beyond. If you get there during a practice session, just keep looking hungrily through the windows with your cameras and they will invite you in! We took a ton of photographs and sent them to their director. What a fun afternoon.

The St. Louis Art Museum

Located in Forest Park by the Zoo
1 Fine Arts Drive • St. Louis, MO 63110
314-721-0072
Free
Yes, cameras are allowed inside! They do request no flashes, or photography of any of the "special events" that might be happening at that time. Otherwise you are free to roam with your equipment. This is such a good place to practice; first, because it's warm in cold weather and secondly, air conditioned in hot weather. You can also check your coat in the winter if you don't want to lug it around. There are lots of **archways**, **hallways**, **reflective light** off the floor, the opportunities are endless!

Skate Board Arenas

Plan Nine Skatepark
5555 St. Louis Mills Blvd, Suite 373 • Hazelwood, MO 63042
314-227-5294

We have visited two inside skatepark arenas, so far, and both were fascinating and provided plenty of **action shots**. Do these young people have no fear?? Do they not break bones?? Eeeeek.

This place is at the east end of the St. Louis Mills Mall, right next to the ice hockey ring where the Blues practice. We checked in with the manager of the Skatepark and asked if we could go inside, rather than hang around outside of the Arena. The fencing is hard to see through. He said, *"Sure, but you have to wear helmets."* Of course the helmets are made for (ah hum) younger people. It's not like we didn't stand out enough, being the oldest people in the building, now we had to look even more dorky with these small, little white egg-shell-looking things precariously perched on the back of our heads! "Hey dude, surf's up." (Well we don't know any skateboard language).

It didn't take the kids long to decide to show off and boy could they do some tricks. We had cameras and tripods and it took us a while to get the hang of their moves, but they started hollering at us to "watch this" ...

Ramp Riders

2324 Salena • St, Louis, MO 63104
314-776-4025

The second place we hit during a blistery, cold day was located in the Soulard area: www.rampriders.net or www.myspace.com/rampridersskatepark

This place advertises "indoor ramp park for: skateboards, BMX bikes, MTB bikes, inline skates, scooters (I don't think they mean hover-arounds, which are my speed), and heelys." Don't ask us what "heelys" are.

I should mention that it's a little difficult finding this place because it looks like (and it is) part of an **old warehouse**. You enter by the dumpster (no kidding) and the door leads up to the second floor. You can hear the skaters from here.

Neither place charged us admission (What? They didn't think we wanted to skate???). And, this place didn't require us to wear a dorky helmet. Whew. We could be "cool and hip" once again.

We liked the character of this old building because it still retained its warehouse feel, including lots of **windows** and **natural lighting**.

Missouri History Museum
5700 Lindell Blvd • St. Louis, MO 63112
314-746-4599
Free
Again, as with the Art Museum, there is no problem bringing in cameras and/or tripods (no flashes). There is also a place toward the back where you can hang coats if needed.

Many of the exhibits (not all by far) are covered with Plexiglas (the bane of a photographer's existence); however, if it isn't scratched, put your lens right up next to it and sometimes this works. You will obviously have to have a large aperture setting and/or slow shutter speed so best to have a tripod if there is something you really want a picture of.

St. Louis Public Library
1415 Olive Street • St. Louis, MO 63103
314-539-0359
Free
This beautiful building, built around 1908 is gorgeous inside and the staff welcomes photographers (no flash), tripods ok, as long as they are not bothering the patrons. Patron is a charming, quaint old word they use meaning customer. It

sounds so dignified, doesn't it?

There are various places to park, but right in front is the most convenient; however, there are parking meters that eat coins voraciously so be sure to have plenty of change. On Sundays only the newer, more modern building is open.

Cathedral Basilica
4431 Lindell Blvd • St. Louis, MO 63108
314-373-8200
Free
A must see if you love **neo-Byzantine architecture** and it also has the largest collection of **mosaics**. Cameras and tripods are allowed. While we didn't see any signs for "no flashes" we would rather err on the side of caution in case lightening strikes or something. Obviously, we weren't there during any services.

Union Station
1820 Market Street • St. Louis, MO 63103
Free
Another fabulous **old train station** and we have never seen any signs warning against "no flashes." Obviously this was once the home to bustling trains and passengers; now, unfortunately, a few shops, but a lot of empty ones. We do understand plans are in the works for renovation. However, the main hall is still a great place to take photographs and there is still a hotel in operation. Occasionally, someone has grumbled about a tripod, but it's not like the place is overly crowded.

Jewel Box
Forest Park
Wells and Summit Drive • St. Louis, MO
314-531-0080
This is a **totally glass building**, beautiful in and of itself, with **outside lily ponds** blooming during their season. We were there very early one hot summer morning and the volunteers

were cleaning out the ponds and told us if we wanted, we could actually get in the water for up-close shots. We didn't have old tennis shoes with us that day or we would have been right in there. The bottom is concrete and a little slimy, to say nothing of slippery so you want to be careful with your camera, too. You'll dry out. A camera? Not so much.

If you choose to go inside (open all year long) they are now charging $1/each admission. It's also a good place to take clients for portrait sessions, as the light is wonderful.

The Old Courthouse
11 North 4th Street • St. Louis, MO 63102
314-655-1700
Free
A simply gorgeous **old building** and home of the famous Dred Scott slave case. You can take cameras and tripods. I didn't see any warnings about "no flash." There are also many **staircases**.

St. Louis City Hall
1200 Market Street • St. Louis, MO 63103
314-622-4800
The main area of City Hall is the 45-foot by 65-foot square atrium (called the **Rotunda**) reaching four stories in height, encircled by balustrade **balconies** on each of the upper three stories that overlook the ground floor. The floors are white Italian marble. Leading from the first floor lobby to the second floor is a grand **marble staircase**. The corridors include **cast-iron steps**, oak trim, marble, wainscoting and **ornamental ceilings**.

This building is not open during the weekends.

There is also a great **old clock** on the outside, which has a Missouri pink granite that contrasts with pink-orange Roman brick on the upper floors and buff color sandstone trim around the window openings, and the roof is burgundy-red clay tiles.

This is a very unusual piece of **architecture**, with many ornamental dormers.

City Hall
University City
6801 Delmar • University City, MO 63130
314-862-6767
Free
There is a fabulous staircase right inside the front door. We spent quite a bit of time inside and we did use flashes, as well.

This is a 5-story octagonal tower building constructed in 1903/1904.

Purina Farms
200 Checkerboard Drive • Gray Summit, MO 63039
314-982-3232
wwwpurinafarms.com
Free (reservations are best)
This is really a farm and we mention it here because they have several great indoor buildings (**barn**, **cat house**, **dog** show arena). It's a great place for kids and adults as well.

Kirkwood Train Station
110 West Argonne Drive • Kirkwood, MO 63122
314-984-8617
The historic Kirkwood Train Station sits in the middle of historic downtown Kirkwood, across from the oldest Farmers' Market in Missouri. Shops, restaurants, fun. This is another great indoor place with plenty of photo ops; or you can step outside and see the trains coming.

TOPIC INDEX

Topic	Page	Additional Information Not Mentioned in Book
— A —		
Action Shots		Rodeos and Horse Shows: www.missourirodeo.com or www.mohorseshows.com; for Illinois www.rodeoz.com or www.Illinoishorseshow.com
Aquarium	101	City Museum in Downtown St. Louis
Altar	43	
Alligators	46	
Amish	120-124	Jamesport, Mo; Bolling Green, Mo
Angles	110	
Animals (barnyard)	61	Suson Park (St. Louis County)
Antiques	73, 104, 113	
Architecture	70, 74, 87, 161, 165, 167	St. Charles, Mo
Arches	82	
Archways	49-50, 163	
Artists – Spray Paint	80	
— B —		
Bank Vaults	161	
Barns	53, 75, 87, 90, 113, 121	Belleville, Il past Eckerts on Highway 15; Highway 109 on road to Babler State Park, St. Louis County; Highway 21 (South into Jefferson County, Mo)
Barn with Mill Stone	62	
Barges	81, 95	St. Genevieve, Mo; St. Charles Mo; Alton, Illinois
Bed and Breakfasts	91	
Benches (old, new, painted)	61, 91, 124	
Birds	97	Wildlife Bird Sanctuary, Valley Park, Mo.
Black River	31	
Blacksmith Barn	124	
Bluebells (flowers)		Castlewood State Park (Ballwin, Mo. in May)
Booths (antique)	83	
Booths (photo)	143	
Brick Fireplace	61	
Bridges	35, 104	
Bright Colors/Lights		City Garden, downtown St. Louis, Mo in the evening; local carnivals/festivals; Lumiere Casino (St. Louis, Mo) outside;
Broken Windows	38	
Buggies	120-122, 124	

Topic	Pages	Location
Buildings (old, deserted)	39, 77, 101, 109	Labadie and before Labadie on Highway T (Missouri)
Buses	90, 161	
Butterflies		Butterfly House, Faust Park in Chesterfield, Mo; Shaw Nature Preserve off of Highway 44 and Gray Summit
C		
Caboose	87	St. Genevieve, Mo at Ferry Landing; Valley Park, Mo; Frontier Park in St. Charles, Mo.
Candy	71-74	St. Charles, Mo
Cars (old, junk)	52	Highway 67 south of St. Louis off of Highway 55
Carnivals		www.festivalsvisitmo.com; www.riverfronttimes.com; www.stlouistoday.com; www.fairsandfun.com/Illinois; www.countyfairgrounds.net/Illinois; www.midwest-carnivalshows.com
Carousel		Faust Park, St. Louis County
Cats (domestic)		Purina Farms at Gray Summit, Mo (see the Cat House there!)
Cats (wild)	85-86	
Celebrity Alerts	33, 78	
Cemeteries	53, 64, 75, 77, 89	Augusta, Mo; Bellefontaine Cemetery, 4947 W Florissant Ave, St. Louis, Mo; Jefferson Barracks, St. Louis County; In Illinois: Red Bud, Waterloo and Columbia
Centennial Farm	53	
Chains (old, big rusted)	81	
Chapel	43	
Chess Set (big)	91	
Chickens	46	Suson Park, St. Louis County and Marthasville Fall Festival, Marthasville, Mo
Chipped Paint	82	
Churches	53, 62, 64, 75, 77, 82, 89, 104, 106, 113	
Circus	162	
Clothesline	137	
Clock (big)	166	
Coca-Cola Memorabilia	74	
College Campus	106	
Color	52, 68, 70, 80	
Colored Candy	74	
Company Store	58	
Country Roads (gravel)	121	

Countryside . . . . Highway 94 from 40/64 and 94 all the way to Hermann, Mo, St. Louis County
Court Houses (old). 95
Covered Bridge . . . . 62, 117 Jackson, Mo
Cows . . . . 123 Labadie, Mo and Highway 21 South
Craft/gift Shop. 68, 91
Creeks. . . . . 34-33, 110 Castlewood State Park in Ballwin, Mo; Greensfelder State Park by Eureka, Mo. See Park Listings at end of this Chapter
Crocodiles 46
Cross (huge and white) 109
Curves 110

— D —

Deserted Farm Houses . . . . 35 Belleville, Ill by Eckharts off Highway
Diners. . . . . History Museum in Forest Park, St. Louis, Mo; Manhattan City Diner, Clayton, Mo.
Dogs. 167
Doors (old, unusual). 36, 57, 78, 90
Drive-In Theater. . . . . Highway 21 on way to Ironton, Mo.
Ducks 90, 97

— E —

Eads Bridge 95
Eagles 93, 97, 103
Emus . . . . 46 Cuba, Mo (see Gas Pumps (Antique) below
Equipment. 38, 61, 90, 124
Eras Gone By 81

— F —

Fall Colors 35
Farm Equipment 124
Farm Fields (Land) . . . . 35 Labadie, Washington and New Haven, Missouri
Farm Wagon . . . . 75 St. Charles, Mo (historic Old Main Street); Labadie, Mo; Ballwin, Mo on New Ballwin Road in Castlewood, Mo.
Fences (split rail, old). . . . . 61 Faust Park in St. Louis County; Shaw Nature Preserve in Gray Summit, Mo; Labadie, Mo
Ferris Wheel. 161
Ferries (car) . . . . 87, 103 St. Genevieve, Mo
Fireplaces (old). 61, 63
Fireworks . . . . Downtown St. Louis; local parks
Flowers . . . . 61, 68, 124 Community Gardens for flowers and vegetables – Wildwood, Missouri and St. Louis City on South Broadway
Foot Bridges 104
Front Porches. 68
Fruit Orchards . . . . Eckhardts in Belleville, Il.

G

Gas Pumps (Antique) . . . . Cuba, Mo (huge collection that can be seen from Highway 44) Owner has Furniture Store in town. Just ask Permission and Directions there.

Gears 38

General Store 59, 62, 64, 73, 113

Ghost Lovers . . . . 58 Lemp Mansion in St. Louis City;

Graffiti . . . . 82 South Broadway in St. Louis City

Gravel Roads 31, 35, 69

Great River Road 102-104

Guitar Maker 109

H

Hilly Farm Country 53

Historical 57, 83, 91

Historic Structures 57

Horse and Buggies 121

Horses . . . . Highway T going out to St. Albans, past Wildwood City Hall (Missouri); Valley Mount Ranch on Highway 44, Valley Park, Mo. Must gain permission to photograph.

Houses (old, deserted) . . . 31, 35, 69, 90

I

Industrial sites (deserted) 38

Iron Fences . . . . 78 Soulard Area off Broadway in St. Louis City.

J

Juke Boxes (table top and regular size) . . . . 83 Blueberry Hill in University City Mo.; Manhattan City Diner, Clayton, Mo.

Junkyard 90

K

Katy Trail 68

Kitchen (old) . . . . 62 History Museum in Forest Park (St. Louis City)

Komodo Dragon 46

L

Lavender . . . . www.windingbrookestate.com outside of Eureka, Mo

Lead Mines 38

Lighthouses . . . . 100-109 Old Chain of Rocks Bridge crossing Mississippi River north of St. Louis, off of Riverview Drive. Technically called Water Intake buildings, but they are fabulous stone/architecture and built in 1904 for St. Louis Worlds Fair

Lighting spots (portraits) . . . . Jewel Box in Forest Park (St. Louis City); Missouri Botanical Gardens

Lily Ponds. . . . . Jewel Box and Missouri Botanical Gardens (St. Louis); Shaw Nature Preserve in Gray Summit, Mo; Tower Grove Park (St. Louis City)
Limestone 108, 113, 115, 116, 117
Lions. 46, 85
Llamas . . . . Farm off of Highway 61 between Bloomsdale and Cape Girardeau, Mo
Loading docks (old, deserted). 82
Locks and Dams. 98
Lodges (rustic) . . . . 110 Pere Marquette Park close to Alton, Illinois
Log Cabins 57, 58, 62, 74, 108
Log Church . . . . Cahokia, Il www.holyfamily1699.org
Low Water Concrete Slab Bridges. . . . 35
Lost History Museum 57, 58

— M —

Meramec River. . . . . 47 Sherman Beach which is part of Castlewood State Park off of St. Paul Road in Sherman, Mo.
Mills . . . . 31, 113 Jackson, Mo Hodges Mill along with covered bridge
Mine Machinery 38
Mines (old, lead, deserted) 38
Mississippi River. . . . . . . 80, 87, 100, 115 Old Chain of Rocks Bridge (part of old Route 66) and bike/walking trail across river – St. Louis County
Missouri Eiffel Tower 40
Missouri Pacific Railroad 52
Missouri River. 69, 89
Missouri Wine Country 64
Monkeys. 46
Mosaics 43, 165
Motorcycles 69, 71
Multi-colored rock Sculptures 43
Museum. 39, 57, 58, 104, 124

— N —

Natural Rock Formations 34
Neo-Byzantine Architecture. 165

— O —

Old Buildings. 39, 77, 101, 109
Old Courthouses 95
Old Pianos, Organs 104, 106
Old Rusted Trucks . . . . 87 Labadie, Mo
Old School Desks . . . . 68 School in Columbia, Illinois
Old Windows
. . . . 31, 38, 61, 70, 82, 90, 161, 164
Old Towns 77, 91
Old Village Mercantile. 73
Original Handwritten Ledgers 58

Ornamental Ceilings 166
Ostrich . . . . 46 Cuba, Mo
Outbuildings 70, 113
Outdoor Settings 91
Overnight Road Trip 120
Overlooks. 91, 95 Bloomsdale, Mo off of old 61 which runs parallel to Highway 55; Bluffs at Castlewood State Park in Ballwin, Mo

P

Parks . . . . 40, 51, 104, 110 See page 176 for listing
Peeling Paint 70, 116
People Watching . . . . 47 Central West End in St. Louis City; Soulard Market in St. Louis City off of Broadway
Pelicans 97
Picket Fences. . . . . 78, 104 Faust Park, St. Louis County
Pianos. 104
Planes. . . . . 161 Jefferson Barracks, St. Louis County
Prairie. . . . . 97 Shaw Nature Preserve at Gray Summit, Mo.
Pumpkins . . . . 114 Rombach Farm in Chesterfield, Mo.

Q

Quaint Little Town
. . . . 64, 68, 77, 103, 108, 113 St. Charles, Mo; Labadie, Mo.

R

Railroad Cars 87
Railroad Trestles. . . . . Labadie, Mo; Valley Park, Mo; Sherman Beach (part of Castlewood State Park) off of St. Paul Road in Sherman, Mo
Red Bud Trees 53
Red Color. 57
Red Shed 68
Reptiles 45, 179
Restored Original/Gas Pumps . . . 52, 104 Cuba, Mo.
River Bluffs . . . . 69 Castlewood State Park in Ballwin, Mo; West Tyson Park close to Eureka, Mo;
River Front Areas . . . . Washington and St. Genevieve, Mo; Alton, Ill.
River Towns 100
Rock Bluffs 35
Rock Structures 124
Rock Walls 124
Rock Formations 34, 110
Rolling Hills 64, 89
Rope. 81, 161
Rust (rusty tractors, trucks)
. . . . 11, 38, 40, 68, 81, 87, 90, 116
Rotundas 166

—— S ——

Scenic (Overlooks, Vistas, Views) . . . 31, 34, 43, 53, 68, 69, 87, 89, 91, 95, ... 106, 108, 109, 113, 120, 121, 178
School Bus 161
School House (old) . . . . 62, 64, 104, 124 Columbia, Illinois
Sculptures . . . . City Garden, downtown St. Louis; Laumeier Sculpture Park off Watson Road and Highway 44 St. Louis County
Seagulls 100
Sewing Machine (old) 104
Shawnee National Forest. 108
Sheds 68
Shoe Phone Line 87
Shoe Tree. 87
Shorebirds 97
Skateboarding 161-163
Sky Lift 92
Slides 161
Small White Church 62
Smokehouses. 113
Snakes 46
Snake Skins 45
Split Rail Fences. . . . . 61 Faust Park, St. Louis County
Spray Paint Artists . . . . 80 South Broadway in St. Louis City
Springs (water) 31
Stairways (staircases) . . . . 70, 74, 82, 110, 166 Fort Belle Fontaine, North St. Louis County; Castlewood State Park in Ballwin, Mo
Stone Buildings 82
Stone Foundations. 103
Stone Schoolhouse 64
Stone Walls 104
Storefront 69
Statuary 161
Structures (old, unusual) 40, 49, 57, 58, 115, 116, 124
Sunflowers . . . . 91 Rombachs Farm in Chesterfield, Mo; Defiance, Mo; and the City/Community Garden in Wildwood, Mo by City Hall and movie theater
Swans. . . . . 97 Highway 141 and Clayton Road in lake in front of Shopping Center
Superb Vistas. . . . . Castlewood State Park in Ballwin, Mo. See Park Listings at end of this chapter

—— T ——

Texture. 31, 61, 68, 70, 82, 90, 92
Textured Buildings 61
Telephone Booth . . . . Waterloo, Illinois
Tigers. 46, 85, 86
Towns. 77, 91, 100
Tombstones 78, 89

Trains 52, 95, 161, 165, 167
Train Stations . . . . 165, 167 Kirkwood, Mo
Tree Swing 91
Tunnels. 50, 161
Turtles (huge, real ones). 100

—— U ——

Urban Sites. 82

—— V ——

Valley 113
Village Green 61, 62
Vintage Cars. 52

—— W ——

Warehouses 164
Waterfalls . . . . 130 Eminence, Mo (Rock Falls); Forest Park in St. Louis, Mo
Water Fowl. 97
Water Geyser . . . . East St. Louis, Il. See www.meprd.org/mmmp.html for geyser times
Water Tower. . . . . 110 Around St. Louis City: Grand Water Tower, Bissel Water Tower and Compton Hill Water Tower. The Grand Water Tower is open to the public at certain times, including full moons. www.watertower-foundation.org
Water Wheels. St. Charles, Mo on the side of the Trail Head Restaurant
Weathered Front Doors 78
Wetlands 97
White Picket Fences. . . . . 78 Faust Park in St. Louis County
Wildlife. 35, 45, 90
Wildlife Refuges. . . . . Wolf Sanctuary at Tyson Park, St. Louis County. See Park List at end of Chapter
Wildlife Sanctuaries . . . . See Park List at end of Chapter
Wildlife Preserve 90
Windmill. 124
Windows (old) 38, 61, 82, 90, 161
Wine Country. 64, 65, 87
Wineries. 65, 108
Woodburning Brick Oven 63
Woodchucks. 90

—— Y ——

Yards. . . . . 76 Soulard Area, St. Louis City

—— Z ——

Zip Lines. 47

County/State Parks
Great Photo Ops
Missouri

Park	Address	Photo Ops
Bee Tree	2701 Finestown Road St. Louis, Mo 63129	River Vistas
Castlewood	1401 Kiefer Creek Ballwin, Mo 63021	Meramec river vistas, creeks, wildflowers, staircase, old railroad tunnels under elevated tracks
Creve Coeur Lake	13236 Marine Creve Coeur, Mo 63146	Lake, paths, sailboats, sailboat cove
Faust	15185 Olive Blvd Chesterfield, Mo 63017	Recreated old village, barn, herb gardens, Butterfly House, Carousel, historic governor's house, cemetery
Fort Belle Fontaine	13002 Bellefontaine Rd St. Louis, Mo 63138	River views, staircase, historic fort
Greensfelder	4515 Hencken Rd Eureka, Mo 63069	Foothills of Ozark mountain range, scenic views, creeks, horse trails
Jefferson Barracks	345 North Road St. Louis, Mo 63125	Army post from 1826 to 1946, burial grounds for veterans (flags placed on graves certain times of the year), great views of Mississippi and bridge into Illinois
Lone Elk	1 Lone Elk Park Road Valley Park, Mo 63088	Wildlife management area with bison, wild turkey, elk and deer, lake

Simpson Park	Located off of Marshall Rd. in Valley Park, Mo just north of I-44 and east of highway 141	Lake fishing, flat bike trails, model plane flying certain weekends, Wildlife Sanctuary brings in Eagles certain weekends in January/February
Suson	6073 Wells Rd St. Louis, Mo 63128	Working farm and animals plus 3 lakes
Sylvan Springs	300 Halsey Rd St. Louis 63125	Part of Jefferson Barracks mentioned above, skateboarding, BMX Bikes, Scooters and Rollerblades
Tilles Park	9551 Litzsinger Rd St. Louis, Mo 63124	Winter Wonderland Light Display
West Tyson	131 North Outer Road East St. Louis, Mo 63025	Ozark beauty, steep bluffs, Meramec River, some water falls
Wolf Sanctuary	www.endangeredwolfcenter.org 636-938-5900	Call for hours/tours. Times/dates vary
Wildlife Bird Sanctuary	125 Bald Eagle Ridge Road Valley Park, Mo 63088	Birds, Mammals, Reptiles, nature center

DISCLAIMER

Don't Blame Us If It Isn't There

Unfortunately no one asks our permission to tear anything down. Just because someone owns property does that give them the right to tear down a great photo op? Jeezzzz So, we are sorry if you end up at a deserted house/barn/etc. that is no longer there!

HOW TO CONTACT US

Snappin Sistas

www.snappinsistas.com
snappinsistas@gmail.com

Judy Coday
(Cowgirl Judy)
judy_coday@yahoo.com

Nancy Lister
(Bad Nancy)
nancy.lister@yahoo.com

Angie Gellner
(Fearless Angie)
angiegellner@gmail.com

ABOUT THE AUTHORS

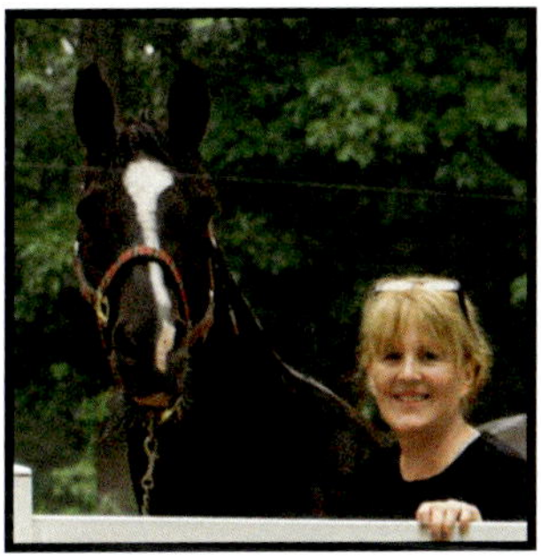

JUDY CODAY was raised in Illinois on a small cattle and horse farm back when they didn't have cell phones and t-v was black and white. Photography has been Judy's other love (besides her husband, Bill) – along with her horses – as long as she can remember. Today she lives with her husband, 2 horses, 2 cats and 1 dog in Ballwin, Missouri. Besides writing this book, she is a photographer and still avid horsewoman. You can contact Judy at judy_coday@yahoo.com.

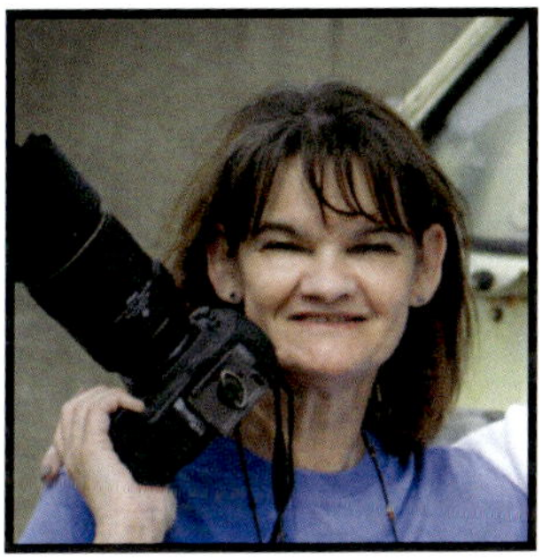

NANCY LISTER is a native Missourian who was raised in St. Louis City. She is a photographer and avid Photoshop user. She loves to travel. Just say the words, "You want to go somewhere?" and she's gone! Her dream is to do more traveling and to sell her photography from her own studio. Nancy lives in Pevely, Missouri with her husband Tom. You can contact Nancy at nancy.lister@yahoo.com.

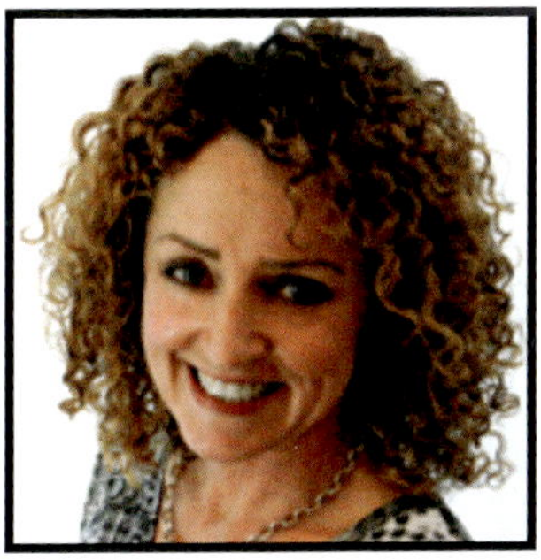

ANGIE GELLNER is also a native Missourian raised in Jefferson County. She is a graphic designer by trade. Her hobbies include running trails, hitting the gym, horseback riding and photographing everything. While she can change her own oil (the kind in a car), don't ask her to iron a shirt! Angie lives in Ballwin, Missouri with her husband David and their two dogs. You can contact Angie at angiegellner@gmail.com.

"What we have here are women, camera snapping women, desperate but determined; with transportation, cameras, spare time & (honestly) NO idea what is going to happen next, traveling through towns in Missouri and Illinois. Yes, they are Out There, with No Restraints on their photo-lust obsession. You can say It's In Them, and it's GOT to come out. So far. any resemblance to Thelma & Louise and their fellow camera-obsessive, loyal friend is merely coincidental, and thankfully has yet to see them drive off that cliff. Now this book, which tells all---we're all better for reading it, tales of small towns, river towns, spread along Missouri & Illinois, along the Mississippi. Women with cameras----it's a photo-prowl."
Tom 'Papa' Ray, DeeJay - The Soul Selector, KDHX-88.1 FM
President/ Vintage Vinyl

I'm not a photographer but I really liked this book. Having lived all my life in Illinois, but working in St. Louis, who knew there were so many different and unusual places to visit so close to home? This is a perfect guide as seen from the eyes of people who have a sense of humor and enjoy our areas from a totally unusual perspective.

Mike Henderson, Respiratory Therapist and "exploration enthusiast"